# Shortcuts to
# JUSTICE

## JOSEPH E. CARTER

Retired Special Agent, ATF

U. S. Treasury

## SSI Publications

D1059490

**Library of Congress Cataloging-in-Publication Data**

Carter, Joseph E.

Shortcuts to Justice

1.Law Enforcement

2. Moonshining, Illicit Distilling

I. title

1999

ISBN 0-9634357-4-4 (Hard cover)

ISBN 0-9634357-5-2 (Soft cover)

99-94516

Published in the United States by
Joseph E. Carter
P.O. Box 1119
Albemarle, North Carolina  28002

Printed in the United States of America
Photographs by various Treasury Agents
Cover design and artwork by SSI Publications

# FOREWORD

Joseph E. Carter enjoyed an illustrious twenty year career in law enforcement. He first served as a police officer in Albemarle, North Carolina, and went on to serve in the Treasury Department as a federal agent. Shortly after he joined the Treasury Department, Mr. Carter's branch became known as the Alcohol and Tobacco Tax Division. Subsequently this branch was named the Bureau of Alcohol, Tobacco and Firearms (ATF).

Mr. Carter volunteered for military service during World War II and entered the service as the war was coming to a close. He transferred from active duty to active reserves in 1950. During the Viet Nam era, he trained more than 1,000 men in riot control and other aspects of police work. He concluded his military career in 1970 as a major in the Army Reserve Command for North and South Carolina.

Since his retirement from ATF in 1973, Joe Carter has let no grass grow under his feet. Presently he is a cattleman and equestrian. He is a well respected member of his community, a successful businessman, college lecturer, author of books, philanthropist and humanitarian.

Joe Carter is a member of a number of distinguished organizations such as the local Fraternal Order of Police, the Retirement Association of the National Association of Treasury Agents, the North Carolina Sheriffs Association, the North Carolina Business Advisory Commission under the N.C. Secretary of State, and the Stanly County Economic Development Commission. He is also one of the very few people in the world to have received an honorary membership in the Navy SEAL team.

In June of 1995, Mr. Carter participated in a film documentary on PBS and TBS entitled "Driving Passion." He spoke of what he calls "revenuing" work, attempting to capture the early liquor runners and their cars. He succeeded more often than not, much to the liquor runners' chagrin. Many of these runners became the early professional race car drivers and many are still involved in the sport today.

Whether lecturing to a college class, speaking at a business forum, speaking through his books to his readers, or simply sitting in your living room, Carter is charismatic and spellbinding without being aware of it. Joe Carter never does anything halfway—it's "damn the torpedoes (or allegators) and full speed ahead."

Joe Carter is truly a legend in his own time.

Lois Hoopes (Seal) Coram, Ph.D., Criminologist
Head of the Department of
Sociology/Criminal Justice
Associate Professor Pfeiffer College

Large N.C. distillery showing elaborate camouflage to avoid detection from the air. Vats contain fermenting mash.

# INTRODUCTION

This book is a sequel to *Damn the Allegators*, published in 1989. It is a factual and shocking account of an elite segment of your "Treasury Men in Action" in the fifties and sixties involved in the destruction of illegal liquor, and the 'warfare' with the criminals responsible for making and distribution of it. It is violent, raw and somewhat profane, but that's the way it was, and to write it otherwise would be depriving the reader of its reality.

Because of two factors, one being that the statute of limitations has run out in some instances, and two, many potential witnesses are now dead, I can now tell some stuff that was originally withheld for obvious reasons.

I was encouraged by many people to write this sequel. *Shortcuts to Justice* illustrates some accidental, coincidental and intentional overlooking of the fine print instructions in many of our legal and constitutional provisions.

Like almost everything else, time and progress has changed many aspects of law enforcement and the pursuit of justice. No longer can a repair invoice for the police car, an insurance policy, or a car title be used as a 'search warrant'. An officer foolish enough to try such a scheme now could risk exchanging his badge number for a prison number. Because of the Fourth Amendment to the Constitution, obtaining a valid search warrant can be so difficult that it is sometimes not worth the effort, especially in the case of commercial crimes of little significance.

A debate about the merits of tactics used 'back then' and modern tactics now employed in law enforcement would be pointless due to modern scientific development of such techniques as DNA comparison, neutron activation process, microwave and laser technology, supersonic communication and other resources. BUT, the modern agents can't possibly be having as much fun as we did!

# Table of Contents

Upright steam boiler still hidden in deep woods. Shed camouflaged with tree branches.

# CAPTAIN BLACK JACK NOLAND

In the early 1950's serving Sheriff Paul E. Herrin in the small North Carolina county of Stanly, I received a telephone call early one morning as the only deputy sheriff that could walk upright, from a citizen reporting the theft of his automobile. Auto theft was rather rare in those days, quite unlike now. Stealing cars seems to be a favorite sport today.

The first action then was to call the local state prison to see if any prisoners had escaped the previous night. "Affirmative," said the superintendent, "we've already caught the son-of-a-bitch. Come on down and question him if you like, but he will never talk. He's serving thirty years now for armed robbery and he won't tell you shit."

I was escorted into the office of the superintendent. After the usual complimentary greetings, he proceeded to tell me how mean, vicious, tough and uncooperative the prisoner was and assured me that I was wasting my time. "I need to question him anyway, for the record." I said.

The superintendent turned to another 'official' and said, "This is Captain Noland, he has just transferred here from Ivy Bluff, the toughest and most notorious prison in the state. He will go with you out to the 'hole' to talk to the son-of-a-bitch."

The 'hole' was just that! About thirty feet deep, and about eight feet in diameter, it was housed over by a windowless masonry building about the size of a large outhouse.

Captain Noland looked like the old-time western movie star, Lash Larue. Powerfully built and dressed totally in black, he did not speak a word until we were inside the building that housed the hole.

He unlocked a steel trap door flush with the floor, turned on a light and uttered the first words that I had heard him say, to a miserable character cowering at the bottom of the hole. "Get your ass up here, boy," he boomed. The prisoner climbed up a stationary ladder and sat on the floor, feet dangling over the hole. Noland took an 18 inch long flapjack from his pocket and tapped it lightly on the palm of his left hand. A 'flapjack' is a weapon made from two thick pieces of leather with a heavy piece of lead sewed within. He then spoke for the second time. "Why did you steal that automobile last night?"

The prisoner snarled, "Fuck you, I didn't steal no car, and I ain't telling you nuthin', you bastard!" The deadly flapjack struck him above the left ear with enough force to drop a buffalo.

Blood spurted everywhere. The poor guy collapsed like a wet dishrag. His moaning was interrupted by Captain Noland who pulled him back to a sitting position. "I asked you a goddam question! Why did you steal that automobile last night?"

In a very weak voice, blood filling his mouth, nose and ears, he replied, "I—I—told you I — I —— didn't —— steal——." SPLAT"... went the flapjack on the man's head again, while I simply stared in shock at the brutal treatment. Blood, more blood! Now the prisoner crumpled on the floor, only partially conscious. Tapping his left hand again with the terrible weapon, Noland listened to the crying for a few minutes until the man regained some awareness, then said, "I'm going to ask you one more time and if you lie to me again, I'm going to finish killing you." Tears mixing with blood and staining his clothes, the prisoner stammered, "Well— I —— I— stole it— to— try to get away...."

"Okay sheriff, you heard his confession, you can go ahead now and get a warrant," Noland growled. I have never again witnessed such a brutal act, by an officer of the law. Being too inexperienced and too young in the job, I didn't know whether to piss in my pants or wind my watch. One thing for sure though, I would never in hell try to prosecute that poor guy for auto theft. So I told Captain Noland, "Well since he's already serving thirty years, I'll just let this case slide."

Only 15 minutes before, a veteran prison executive had solidly assured me that the man would probably die before he would talk, but just this quick, Captain Noland had gotten a "confession!" I only hoped that the prisoner wouldn't die before I could get the hell out of that place!

What an introduction to the technique of interrogating a suspect, for a 23-year old "Assistant Sheriff!" I could only hope that when I got into ATF, things wouldn't be this violent!

# DISORDER IN THE COURT (SORTA)

The nearest thing to a negative experience in professional law enforcement is the profound duty of testifying in court—more specifically the boredom of hours and even days spent waiting to give the testimony we have worked so hard to prepare. But in the long term, all is not wasted. At times the legal activity can become very entertaining.

Being a glutton for good humor, I cannot resist relating some of the hilarious events that actually transpired in the course of some trials. It was one such event that provided me the idea for the title to the first book I wrote, "*DAMN THE ALLEGATORS.*" An old Black gentleman had just been convicted of deadly assault on a neighbor.

"Sam, before I sentence you I want to ask you WHY in the world, after living next door to this man and having been close friends for over twenty years, did you almost kill him with a 2x4?" asked the judge.

"Well Yo' Honah, what would you do if someone called you a Black SOB?" replied Sam.

"Well Sam, you know I can't answer that, because I'm not black."

Pondering this, Sam scratched his head and replied. "Well den, judge, what would you do if somebody called you de kinda SOB you really is? Anyway, I denies the allegations and damns the allegators!"

Said the judge: "Five years, hard labor. Next case."

Many of the following incidents came about through our working with local officers. This sometimes resulted in making criminal cases considered by the federal government as insignificant, but nevertheless allowed by our supervisors in some very special instances.

Such cases were authorized primarily to assist certain credible state or local officers in their efforts to eliminate thorns in their sides such as persistent bootleggers who sell alcohol to children in small amounts. It was the objective of the Federal government to concentrate on so-called major violators who are big threats to the revenue, manufacturing whiskey for sale without paying the federal taxes. Contrary to public opinion, the Fed is not concerned with the morality or immorality of the consumption of alcohol—pay the taxes and let her rip!

"Bring those guilty bastards in this here courtroom so's we can give 'em a fair trial!" shouted an assistant of the trial judge of the N.C. Superior Court to the court bailiff.

\* \* \*

Solicitor: "Your Honor, this is one of those cases involving a weekend neighborhood brawl that Your Honor is burdened with almost each time you hold court."

Judge: "That's all right, Mr. Prosecutor. I'm accustomed to it."

Solicitor: "Well sir, this case involved several people and several incidents of affray. In the interest of saving the court's time, we are calling on all complainants that wish to testify, but as briefly as possible."

Judge: "Call your first case."

After several witnesses testified the most vocal complainant, a Ms Ethel Brown, was sworn in. "They was fightin' and cuttin, cussin' and raisin' hell all over the place," she stated.

Solicitor: "Ethel, tell His Honor if you got cut in the fracas."

Ethel: "Well, suh, Yo' Honah, no-suh, I didn't get cut in the fracas, I got cut up heah just above the fracas," pointing to the area of her abdomen just below her belly button.

\* \* \*

It is doubtful that the following story could be verified, but here it is anyway.

A twelve year old boy was being tried for the crime of rape. His attorney was an attractive lady lawyer. The story concerns the final phase of the trial. She began her plea for a jury determination of 'not guilty' by calling the young defendant to stand beside her and proceeding to withdraw his little male organ. Laying it in her hand she paraded him back and forth in front of the jury.

"Ladies and gentlemen of the jury, the prosecution team has, as usual, allowed the truth to be used rather recklessly in their effort to convict this mere child of the terrible crime of rape. As you can easily see, this is an impossibility. Just look at this little dork, almost the size and innocent appearance of that of an infant."

After several minutes of this unusual demonstration, the young defendant, becoming increasingly uncomfortable, whispered into the ear of the lady attorney, "Hey lady if you don't get your hand off my ding-dong, we're goin' to lose this damn case."

\* \* \*

After being convicted for public drunkenness, Alfred stood before the judge. "This is far from your first case, Alfred," stated the judge. "Fifty dollars or thirty days. Which will it be?" "Well Jedge, that shore is nice of you. I'll take the fifty dollars, I shore can use it!" said Alfred.

\* \* \*

A federal judge is never elected, but rather is appointed for life, and it is the intention of the Congress that, once appointed, he may be forever independent of politics.

One particular defendant was found guilty by a jury in federal court in North Wilkesboro, N.C. Upon presentation of evidence of his long criminal record and sustained reputation of major involvement in the moonshine business, the presiding federal judge sentenced him to seven years in federal prison. When asked if he had anything to say, the defendant replied, "OK, Judge, because of that long sentence, I promise you that neither I, nor any member of my family will ever vote for you again. We always have before, but not any more!"

\* \* \*

Another memorable case in federal court in the mountain area of North Carolina involved a defendant who was considered a 'major violator'. The evidence against him was highly circumstantial and far from overwhelming. Although conviction seemed unlikely, the district attorney agreed to try the case because of the man's record of criminal activity. In this area there was somewhat of a paradox concerning the local people who served on a jury. Almost everyone at the time had some connection with the manufacture of moonshine, being related to, doing business with or being a neighbor of someone actively engaged in it. Therefore it would appear to be very difficult to select twelve individuals who would find a defendant guilty. Such was definitely not the case. Most juries reacted just the opposite and with sufficient evidence would usually convict quickly.

After we had presented our evidence, and after the usual defense tactics had been completed, the jury retired to consider a verdict. Although we were prepared for a verdict of not guilty due to the circumstantial evidence, the jury returned in only 25 minutes with a GUILTY verdict. During a short break after the case, I saw the man who had served as jury foreman in the hallway. Meaning it as a friendly joke, I asked him why it had taken them so *long* to arrive at a verdict. Apparently thinking my question was a serious one, he said: "We argued for a long time about who was going to serve as foreman of the jury."

Once in 1958, after being assigned to the "moonshine capital of the world," I arranged for an area wide aerial search for the many unregistered distilleries that we suspected to be in existence. The three day exercise resulted in the seizure and destruction of over fifty operations in Wilkes County alone. There were large, small, old and new ones. The oldest and most interesting one was located in a building on the premises of a Mr. Purdue who was 77 years old. As "experts" we determined the longevity of the distillery to be over six months. Mr. Purdue was the only person on the scene. The distillery nearly filled the house, which stood at an altitude of about 2,000 feet. The complete mass of vegetation including the shrubbery surrounding the residence was dead, having been killed by the spent mash discharged directly into the yard.

At his trial in U.S. District Court, the old gentleman entered a plea of guilty. The judge, noting his age, asked the defendant if he had a statement to make before being sentenced. Mr. Purdue declined until the judge said, "Well, according to your record you have spent a major portion of your life in prison for committing the same crime, that of making moonshine whiskey. It seems that the sentences you have served before have not taught you anything. I must therefore give you a longer sentence this time. It is the judgment of this court that you be imprisoned for a period of seven years."

At this point, Mr. Purdue decided to make a statement. "Your Honor, I'm seventy-seven years old. I'll never live long enough to serve that sentence!"

"Well, Mr. Purdue," said the judge, "just serve as much of it as you can. We won't hold the remainder against you."

# HELL ON WHEELS —
# RALPH SHEW IN A "HEMI"

He was rough as a cob, mean as a snake; a man ranked as a major violator of the liquor laws. Ralph Shew was considered by law enforcement officers to be a *bona fide* gangster and extremely dangerous—a gun toter.

His base of operations was Mooresville, North Carolina. From there he controlled his massive whiskey manufacturing and distribution empire. Unlike many southern moonshiners whose only crime was illegal whiskey, Shew was suspected of more serious crimes such as extortion and robbery.

He was reputedly a cop hater. More than once he had assaulted officers, both city and state. He also enjoyed the reputation of being a car driver with the ability to compete with any NASCAR star.

Needless to say, he was on ATF's Ten Most Wanted list and was constantly the object of some special investigator's principal efforts. Shew was so cunning and violent that there was little chance to develop information from any of his hirelings. His operation was so large that he employed numerous persons to transport the whiskey to various markets. Sometimes just for the hell of it, he would personally drive the whiskey car.

It was inevitable that Shew's drivers would be caught with a load of whiskey on occasion. When arrested, his employees would never rat on the boss, not necessarily because of loyalty but because they knew Ralph would kill their ass.

Being assigned to other major violators in the eastern part of the state, I only heard of Ralph Shew at conferences and from informers. There were rumors that some local and state officers actually feared him so much they attempted to ignore him, sometimes allowing him safe passage through their area. Then came the fateful day I received a call from my boss in Atlanta.

"Joe, we've got to nail Ralph Shew. Do you think you can do it?"

"My God, boss, you've had a special investigation going on him for years, headed by a first-rate investigator. Do you know how much work I have here?"

"Yeah, I know, but we have another case for that investigator. Besides, we need some new blood to size up this son of a bitch. We think you may be the wild bastard who can come up with a way to nail him."

He sounded sincere but I secretly wondered if he was attempting to assign me a case on which I would fail. Although I admired him very much, I had long suspected he had some kind of problem with me. It is a mystery to me why, as my superior, he seemed envious when I submitted high quality cases for practically every racketeer he assigned me. It seemed he *wanted* me to fail. The irony is that *he* would get the credit. Even so, I accepted the challenge.

Because Ralph Shew operated out of the middle and western part of the state, I moved my activities to Charlotte.

There was a bright side to this since my friend C. Richard Hearn was the group leader in Charlotte. Richard had been transferred there at my request, for his own good, when I was his area supervisor in eastern North Carolina.

I reported to Richard and told him I was assigned to develop a case against Ralph Shew. His only remark was, "Good luck!"

"Will you help me with the case?" I asked.

"I've been receiving a lot of information on his drivers," he answered. "But right now, Joe, I got to check out some information about a still down in the south part of the county. Wanta go with me?"

"Is a pig's ass pork?" I asked.

We drove to a place near the Union County border. We hid the government car and proceeded across country. After creeping through the dark woods we saw the outline of an automobile. It was customary for still operators to station someone in an automobile or a tree to sound a warning if any "laws" were sighted.

I sneaked up to the car and suddenly beamed my flashlight on the back seat.

A man and a woman were there, very close and mostly naked. "What are you doing, friend?" I asked.

"Just out here making love to my wife," he responded.

"Naw, you can't be out here in the boondocks, 15 miles from nowhere, making love to your own wife."

"Didn't know it was her till you put that light in here," he replied sheepishly.

That night's reconnaissance didn't produce anything other than a little excitement. On the way back, Richard commented, "Tomorrow night I'm to meet an informer who swears some big bastard from Wilkes County has a monster still in a barn on a farm in Union County. Are you game to go along?"

Again I replied, "Is a pig's ass pork?"

About midnight the following night Richard and I, burdened by what felt like 100 pounds of equipment on our backs, dropped off an undercover vehicle and hit the woods. After what seemed like a 30-mile forced march we finally came to a small clearing.

After Richard's call of the whippoorwill signal, a huge, rough, tough looking man in his thirties appeared seemingly from nowhere.

"Joe, this is Jerry 'Hercules' Dawson. He's so damn mean he can hardly stand himself. He's big in the booze business. He has furnished me a lot of valuable information. Between us, we have provided the warden with some roomers.

"I would never introduce him to any other agent. He'll let you know up front that if you ever screw him up or fail to use the utmost caution in keeping his identity secret, he will gladly kill you. There have been a few people who double-crossed him in the past. Some of those developed the habit of turning up dead.

"Just handle him right and you'll be delighted with him."

I looked him over real good. He was well over six feet tall and built as sturdy as a Belgian horse. He looked strong enough to have muscles in his shit.

"I'm very pleased to know you, Jerry. But I must say that if I was as big as you, I would hunt grizzly bears with a fly swatter."

"Well, Joe, glad to know you, too. There's plenty of little bears out there that's about your size."

Already I liked this man. "Know any of the big boys up in the mountains—you know, in Wilkes County?" I asked.

"I know most of 'em. Who do you want first?"

"How about Ralph Shew?" was my reply.

"I know him well. You after him?"

"Sure am," I said.

"Damn if you ain't big game hunting. Ralph Shew is a bad ass, and you shore as hell will find out he ain't going to be no pushover.

"The son of a bitch won $1500 off me a couple of years ago with his Plymouth Hemi. He brought me 20 cases of 'shine in that goddamn Plymouth. He saw my flathead Ford and started bragging about how he could outrun me. We bet $1500 on a 30-mile race.

"We started out at my farm. He plays dirty racing and damn near everything else he does. If you don't watch him close when he brings you whiskey, he'll shortchange you.

"Anyway, that damn Hemi was hell on wheels. Mostly we raced over dirt roads. Me and my Ford flathead did good over halfway. Ralph kept dust in my face and acted like he was going to ram me and knock me off the road—you know, just like you bastards try to do when you chase us.

"After about 25 miles, my Ford started to overheat and it slowed me down.

"I'll have to hand it to him though, the son of a bitch can flat drive a car. It's a wonder he ain't killed somebody. He'll run through a stoplight or stop sign at over a hundred and not look anywhere but straight ahead."

Jerry's description of Ralph Shew was compatible with the many tales I had heard from both sides of the fence in our ongoing war with moonshiners. Richard and Jerry were both right. Shew was a bad ass. They had convinced me. My biggest concern was that it would be difficult to develop valuable informers who would rat on him without fearing for their lives.

One thing for sure, we were fortunate to have such a valuable informer as Jerry. He was no hireling for other violators but a large operator in his own right.

He was not the conventional informer who provided information for nominal rewards. His concept of business management was to reduce or eliminate serious competition, most especially such dangerous competition as the notorious Shew, whom he suspected of hijacking whiskey.

"What the hell are you guys doing with those big backpacks? Going on a month's camping trip?"

"If that's what it takes," replied Richard. "After all, you're supposed to show us a big still tonight, aren't you?"

"It's there all right. It's in a big barn on a farm no more than a mile from right here. I found out who the big man is that owns it. He's Bud Williams from Wilkes County. He said things got too hot for him up there."

"I'm familiar with that. We caught him when I was stationed there. He's probably out on parole or probation by now," I said.

"Yeah, that's what he told me all right. He's gonna be mighty cagey. Sure won't be wantin' to go back to the pen. I don't believe you'll be seeing him near the still—most likely just his hired hands," explained Jerry.

With Jerry leading the way we struggled through thick trees and underbrush for over an hour. Suddenly we came to the end of the woods and saw a large open field. We were on top of a rather high hill. From there we could see a house and some buildings including a large wooden barn.

"Look to the left end of the barn—the end opposite from the house—and you can see some big round objects. That's the boilers. They're fired by kerosene pressure—gun type burners. The outfit is so damn big it fills up the barn and runs over to the outside."

Burners like the ones he described make a roaring sound similar to a jet airplane. There was no sound coming from them, indicating that the distillery was not in operation.

We were about 400 yards away and looking down on the scene from a higher level. We could see no lights nor hear anything out of the ordinary.

"Jerry, you stay put," I said. "Richard and I will sneak down the hill and into the barn to see when the mash will be ready to run. How about any possible guards or watchdogs?"

"The only people living in the farmhouse is the three still hands that Williams moved in there when he rented the farm. They're pretty young and they may be gone home till the still's ready. I don't think they got any dogs here," he said.

Richard and I quietly stalked the scene, being extremely careful not to leave any telltale tracks. We stopped constantly to look and listen for any indication that anyone was at the scene.

It is amazing how cunning professional moonshiners are when it comes to security and avoidance of detection. It is very difficult for even a veteran agent to successfully find, examine, and leave intact a distillery for later investigation. It is practically unheard of for an untrained person. More often than not, on the second visit agents will find the distillery abandoned. If the operators find one strange footprint, one item misplaced or anything suspicious, they will suddenly find it necessary to be somewhere else. In other words, they will haul ass!

One common trick is to stretch black sewing thread across a path, road or other access. The thread is invisible, especially at night when most raids are conducted. When officers approach the still, they will inadvertently break the thread. Every time the violators go back to the still, they first scout the area to see if any of their traps has been sprung.

One especially resourceful tactic is stretching the black thread across the access route at a height so as to be struck by an intruder at the shins. The violators will deliberately break the thread, leaving each end on the ground. The idea is to cause the officers to believe they caused the break. The officers, hoping to preserve their secret knowledge of the location of the distillery, proceed to tie the thread back together. A deer or other animal could break the thread but would be unlikely to tie it back.

We found no one at the still. The thing was so large it completely filled the barn, which was much bigger than it first appeared. The mash, contained in 40 large 400-gallon fermenters, was prime to be distilled.

We found an old red truck parked outside with a large quantity of new fruit jars ready for the finished product. I marked the under structure of the truck in case we needed to identify it later.

We returned to Jerry and made future plans to meet with him. After he left, we constructed a blind at the tree line overlooking the scene below. We gathered brush that blended well with the trees and placed it to conceal us and camouflage our position. From there we had an excellent view including the east side and both ends of the big barn. We could also see the driveway that would be used by any vehicles coming to the still.

We had an excellent 35 mm camera equipped with a special powerful Meade telescopic component. The equipment was capable of making clear photographs of persons and objects even from our vantage point 400 yards away. If any activity transpired during the night, with any luck at all we could sneak right up to the barn and see what was going on.

Richard and I made camp. It was now time to cook dinner. Cooking dinner on extended surveillance of whiskey stills consists of silently opening cold cans of Beanee Weenies, saltines and whatever is available to drink. We called the delicious morsels "still rations." The military people called them "C rations." I have seen the time when our still rations tasted so good that, had we brought along a French chef who was equally hungry, he would have died with envy.

There was not enough night left to sleep. Nevertheless, we had many ways to make the hours bearable during the seemingly endless waiting for action. With Richard along, there was never a dull moment.

About 10:00 a.m. an old black Ford pickup truck turned off the main road, proceeded down the driveway past the house and stopped at the east end of the barn. With binoculars I watched two men remove a canvas covering from the bed of the truck. They began unloading cases of fruit jars and bags of sugar and carrying them into the barn.

Near the front of the truck was a large steel tank-like object, apparently to be used as an additional steam boiler. One of the men moved the truck to the old dwelling house. Fortunately he parked it where the license was plainly visible to us and our camera.

After photographing everything in sight, I looked for the second man. Soon he walked out of the barn and looked closely at the ground, undoubtedly looking for tracks or any sign that might indicate some intruder (revenuer) had paid a visit. Then to our dismay he slowly walked up the hill, constantly staring in our direction. I could not believe this man could see through our elaborate camouflage. Nevertheless, he continued slowly up the open field directly toward us.

Richard whispered, "The SOB is probably looking for tracks."

"No," I said, "he's not looking at the ground, he's looking up here at the wood line."

He approached within fifty feet and stopped. He appeared to stare even more intently. From that distance he surely would see us. If he had discovered us in the beginning then why in hell did he continue to approach? Then suddenly, he did see something he didn't like.

Still, the guy played it cool. He didn't panic and retreat back down the hill in full flight. He did walk briskly back to the house, however.

Richard and I could not discern just what brought him up there in the first place. We realized that if the operation was hot there would be no possibility of rushing down to seize it. We already had enough photos and evidence to make a known case.

The bureaucrats we worked for lived and survived on known cases. They needed to tell Congress at budget time that "we made x number of cases with a high degree of arrest of the principals."

We knew from long experience that the workers at a distillery were paid peanuts for their efforts. The brains, the white collar violators, would not haul materials or operate the distillery but would provide the financing and distribution of the finished product.

In about five minutes the man who approached us quickly left the farmhouse with another man in the same truck containing the large tank.

We immediately alerted an agent in a radio car. Deciding that the still was hot I instructed the agent to apprehend the vehicle, arrest the occupants and let us know immediately. We had little hope that he would ever see the truck since there were many routes it could take.

We examined the distillery and its premises thoroughly but found no ready-made evidence of the identity of the owners and operators. We did gather certain material of interest that might—just might—amount to something.

One item was a crumpled invoice from Midland Oil Company for 200 gallons of fuel oil and more importantly for a 500-gallon steel tank such as the one on the truck. The invoice was made out to Robert Morris. We later determined that Robert Morris was a fictitious name.

We retrieved scrapings of a black substance from a tank at the distillery. These samples were taken from the openings where pipes screwed into the tank. Apparently the substance was designed to be a joint sealer.

Then we hauled ass out of there. It was daylight and much easier to negotiate the rough terrain. Being a natural born fast walker, I stopped occasionally to wait for Richard to catch up. At one point I looked behind me and didn't see him, but before I had time to call out, I heard a terrible scream. What in hell, I thought. Did he fall into an old well or step in a bear trap? I ran back and found him sitting on the ground, holding his crotch.

"What's wrong, Richard?" I asked.

"Did you see that goddamn electric fence?" he demanded.

"Yeah, I just stepped over it, why?"

"Well, I should have believed the guy who told me you should never piss on an electric fence. Today when I came up to the fence, I thought he was full of shit. So I pissed on the fence and damn, Joe, the electric current almost killed me. I ain't never felt nothing like that before! It almost knocked my ball plumb out of its sack! And I really believe I got a second circumcision."

During the hours-long march out of the wilderness, a wonderful radio message broke through. It was our backup agent informing us he had apprehended the truck with two men in it!

It had headed up U.S. 21, a busy road directly into Charlotte. The backup agent was Stanley Noel, a first class agent who was radical enough to be matched up with such people as Richard Hearn and me!

On the radio I asked Stan to delay releasing the men on bond until we could meet him at the county law enforcement building and interview them. As usual, Stan needed no further instructions.

Another agent picked us up and took us to the law enforcement center. Stan was there with the two people we had seen at the distillery.

The younger one was undoubtedly the one who came up the hill to our hiding place. After reading him his constitutional rights I proceeded to question him about his trek up the hill. He said he never suspected we were there and that he was attracted by the reflection of a piece of metal. When he got close to us he knew something was not right.

He did admit he was from Wilkes County but lied about who he was working for. He swore he did not even know Bud Williams.

We went over the seized truck with a fine toothed comb. There were numerous fingerprints of both defendants but none belonging to Bud Williams.

The following week I went to the Midland Oil Company with the invoice. I interviewed the two owners and obtained sworn statements from both. I showed them color photos of the truck and the large steel tank, and several mug shots of Dwight "Bud" Williams.

Both men identified the person who had purchased the tank and several hundred gallons of fuel oil as the man in the photograph, namely Bud Williams. They said the tank in our photograph was the same size and type Williams had purchased from them.

Although they identified the mug shot of Williams, it would not be sufficient evidence to prosecute him. Therefore it was necessary to devise a scheme for the two owners of the oil company to see Williams in person. If they could identify him that way, we had a case! Or we'd be well on our way toward making one!

Richard and I conferred. We were in a dilemma. "We could get a court order with subpoenas for the oil company owners, have an assistant district attorney meet with them and question them under oath," Richard suggested.

"Bull shit, Richard. We do that and they'll tell us to go fuck a football," I told him.

I thought we should lobby the two good citizens to go with us to North Wilkesboro and somehow let them see Williams in person.

Then it dawned on me. Williams was on federal probation and paroled from prison. I had arrested him years before for possession of a monster still in the basement of his beautiful brick home facing U.S. Highway 421 in eastern Wilkes County.

That distillery filled the basement and was operated for a very long time. We seized the total premises—that is, the house, the land on which it stood, all fixtures, even the clothing and food inside. This was the decision of my supervisor. I was a rookie at the time but the experience made such an impression on me that I remember it in detail.

The incident added to my understanding of what is feasible and what is not worth the effort in enforcing the law.

The seizure of Williams' home was entirely legal. The process is complicated and expensive to the U.S. government, however.

In such a seizure, agents must effect a detailed inventory of every item seized. Thereafter, everything is stored in a bonded warehouse or guarded on site 24 hours a day by full time agents. Advertisements are run in local newspapers as to the sale at public auction. This is done several times, with notices being displayed in the local courthouse. The process requires about 90 days. An auctioneer is contracted to conduct the sale, adding to the cost of seizing the property.

In the Williams case there were hundreds of people at the sale. The house and land were probably worth $80,000. The federal officials assumed the property would bring a good price.

The auctioneer, who was to be compensated with a percentage of the proceeds, went all out attempting to get a premium price. Over and over he praised the location and attractiveness of the home. Then he opened the subject for bids.

In the beginning, there were no bids. On and on, the auctioneer proclaimed the potential bargain at hand. No bids!

After about 30 minutes of pleading, in desperation the auctioneer put the property on the block for any offer.

For some time no one spoke. Then from the rear of the crowd, a soft voice was heard: "$25.00 for the place." No one raised the ante!

At that point it became clear that to seize such property in an area like Wilkes County, where practically everyone was either involved in, related to or sympathetic with the commercial crime of making whiskey, was a complete waste of time and taxpayers' money.

It was simple. Everyone in the area would join in a silent conspiracy to refuse to bid, allowing the owner to buy back his property for $25.00 or a relative or friend to buy it for him.

As a result Bud Williams never had to move from his home. He did go to prison for a few years and was eventually paroled and released to serve a five year probationary sentence.

It was very dangerous for him to continue boot-legging. If caught he could be returned to prison to serve out the old sentence, in addition to any new charges.

This was the reason he moved his operation from Wilkes County to Union County, where he was not known.

Richard agreed with my plan. We went back to visit our friends at Midland Oil Company. They agreed to go with us to North Wilkesboro.

"How the hell are we gonna get Bud Williams to let them see him?" Richard asked.

"He won't even know they saw him."

"How?" he asked.

"Well, since the son of a bitch is on probation, we'll get the U.S. probation officer in Wilkes County to order him to come to his office for a routine report. Our witnesses will be concealed behind a screen where they can get a darn good look at him."

"Brilliant," Richard said.

"Of course," I agreed.

The plan worked like a charm. Robert Tripplet, an able U.S. probation officer with Williams as a client (probationer), was more than willing to cooperate with us. He had reason to believe Bud Williams was back in the moonshine business but had no proof.

Our friends from Midland Oil were placed in an adjoining office equipped with a one-way mirror. They positively identified Dwight "Bud" Williams as the man who had purchased the fuel oil and the large metal tank.

In their statements, both said that Williams came to their place of business, not in the red truck we had seized at the distillery, but in a black 3/4 ton Ford pickup truck.

Having probable cause now to arrest Williams, I followed him from the probation office. He went across the street to the black Ford pickup and opened the door. I arrested him and seized the truck. In the glove compartment I found a two pound can of joint sealer, a black substance that appeared identical to the compound I had found at the distillery.

Naturally, Williams denied any connection with the Union County still, period. He was a hard core violator and we didn't expect to get any admission from him about anything.

The can of joint sealer I took from his truck was what we were gambling on! The name and location of the manufacturer of the sealer were on the can. I wrote to the company and asked them to send another two pound can, which they did.

Then I forwarded the scrapings we took from the boiler, a sample from the partial can seized from Williams' truck and the full can provided by the manufacturer to the ATF laboratory in Atlanta. I requested a comparison of the samples by Neutron Activation Process, a scientific way to positively determine the relativity of almost any substance.

The report of that comparison was significant because each batch manufactured by the company would invariably exhibit unique chemical characteristics. The contents of the new can provided by the company were not quite identical to those of the partial can seized from the truck, *but* the scrapings from the distillery and the substance found in the can in Williams' truck were declared absolutely identical. Needless to say, this was overwhelming evidence that Bud Williams was involved in the Union County distillery over 100 miles from his normal area of operation.

The U.S. District Attorney agreed with Richard and me that this case should be used to revoke Williams' parole and probationary sentence rather than obtain new indictments. After all, our evidence meant he had seven years staring at him.

Bud Williams appeared before a federal judge for violating the conditions of his federal probation. He hired the best and most expensive law firm in the area.

The judge announced that based on the recommendation of the U.S. Attorney he would consider the guilt or innocence of Williams in the pending case while hearing the evidence pertaining to this case.

Normally a probationer or parolee knows he has very little chance to avoid prison once he has screwed up. Consequently he does not put up an expensive legal fight.

Such was not Williams' nature. His attorneys defended him diligently for months, utilizing three court terms and appearing in three separate divisions of the western judicial district of U.S. court. The defense dragged out every conceivable legal weapon, causing us to have to testify over and over to each item of evidence.

The U.S. Attorney conducted a brilliant prosecution which ultimately resulted in the judge ordering Williams' five year probationary sentence revoked. He also sentenced him to five additional years.

This may have been the most important probation violation hearing in recent history due to its length, the notoriety of the defendant, the circumstances and the sophistication of the evidence.

Richard and I later received copies of the best commendation letter either of us had ever received. It was directed to our regional chief of enforcement in Atlanta and was authorized by the U.S. District Attorney. The chief forwarded a copy and wrote an additional letter of commendation of his own, relating to our work in this case.

In those days the hierarchy of ATF was not known to be rapid in patting its agents on the back. We kept them nervous with our unorthodox methods, to say nothing of some of our off-duty celebrations.

Meanwhile, back to the bad man, Ralph (Plymouth Hemi) Shew. After all, he was my assignment and current mission.

After the Williams hearing and a couple of days of self-congratulation, Richard and I spent several days catching up on the past due goddamn unnecessary government reports. Then we settled down to plan how we could make a case on bad ass Ralph Shew.

"Since the son of a bitch is a gun toting cop hater, maybe we'll get a chance to shoot 'im," I suggested.

"Fine, but we really can't count on that. Besides you know that if we did, we'd pay for it with a ton of paperwork. We'd probably be grounded for months while the ass-kissing internal affairs headhunters tried to hang us for doing our jobs," Richard responded.

"Well, fill me in on what you know about his drivers," I said.

Richard had compiled a list of haulers he had arrested since being assigned to Charlotte. Some of those named were reported to be in the employ of Ralph Shew.

Only one caught my serious attention. He was Donald Adkins, a slim young man from the moonshine capital of the world, namely Wilkes County! Having served two tours in that area, I recognized his name and face from a mug shot.

Richard had a rather weak circumstantial case going. He had seized 150 gallons of moonshine in Gaston County at the home of an elderly black widow.

He arrested her and succeeded in gaining her cooperation. When she looked through a mug shot file she identified Donald Adkins as the person who brought the booze and who paid her $20 per week for the use of her house to store it.

Richard showed me her sworn statement reflecting the driver's identity and many details including the type and color of the whiskey car—a black 1960 tri-power Pontiac.

This was a big break. I had arrested Adkins at a moonshine still while stationed at North Wilkesboro. I had convinced the federal judge to give him a lengthy prison term but to suspend it in favor of five years federal probation. Adkins had promised to provide us assistance by furnishing information to help develop criminal cases on other, more important violators. In other words, we would use a small fish to catch big ones.

I was transferred to another post before I was able to follow up on the potential advantage of using Adkins. I only hoped he was still on probation. If he was, we had a much better chance of convincing him to cooperate with us in nailing the big bad ass, Ralph Shew!

A quick inquiry with the federal court revealed Adkins was still on probation. He was under restrictions to remain gainfully employed, not violate *any* state or federal laws and not associate with anyone of bad or questionable character.

I went home to my regular post of duty for the weekend. I called the investigator who had tried to nail Ralph Shew for five years. He didn't know Adkins, but after I described him and the whiskey car he became excited and eager to help.

"I'm damn sure the SOB is Ralph's number one driver. I've received information on a driver and car of that description many times. The driver lives in Wilkes County and this car is just one of many belonging to Shew."

No agent or officer of the law should take the liberty of disturbing another officer's investigation without his permission and cooperation. Richard had made the case against the elderly widow and obtained her sworn statement implicating Adkins.

Back in Charlotte on Sunday, I called Richard at home to ask if he would meet with me that day. "You bet! Pick up a car*toon* of Falstaff and come on over."

Richard and Sue were in the middle of one of their not so rare disagreements. Being a very close friend to both, I was accustomed to this.

After a few rounds of good-natured insults, Sue said, laughing, "You renegades get down to business. I have a bunch of test papers to grade."

"Richard, I have a serious proposal for you," I said. "I'm sure Adkins is hauling booze for Ralph Shew. Now, it's entirely up to you. You made the big seizure in Gaston County and arrested the old lady who identified Adkins. You will have to agree with my plan or we won't even try it.

"In my opinion your case against Adkins is not likely to succeed. Her testimony, in the unlikely event she will testify in court, would be her word against his. While I was in Raleigh this weekend I made some calls. Adkins is still on federal probation so it can be revoked with much less direct evidence than it would require to convict him in the new case.

"Another good thing is that when I arrested the bastard in Wilkes County years ago, he promised to become a valuable informer if I would ask the federal judge to give him a suspended sentence. This would put him on federal probation instead of sending him to prison. I was able to arrange it *but* I was transferred to the other end of the state and never communicated with him again.

"Now, I'm asking you to consider this. Would you be willing to sacrifice your case and use the evidence to show him the danger of having his probation revoked unless he is willing to set up Ralph Shew?"

Without hesitation, Richard blurted, "Do you have to ask? If that ain't a good bet, we won't find one!"

"Good. Now here's how we'll work it. I've got the description of several of Shew's vehicles. I'm familiar with the many routes his drivers use between North Wilkesboro and Charlotte. Our biggest problem in the first phase will be to intercept one of those cars—hopefully driven by Adkins—on his way back empty to Wilkes. If I jump him on his way to deliver the booze he'll run like hell!

"You know I couldn't catch him in his souped-up hot rod liquor car with me driving that goddamn government purchased Mickey Mouse mechanical miscarriage called an automobile. (I once told the boss that if that thing was human it couldn't catch the clap in a Mexican whorehouse.) If I'm lucky enough to spot him when he's empty he'll probably stop without a chase. I figure he'll travel to Charlotte or Gastonia during heavy traffic time, mixing with the people going to work on the second shift.

"Now if you'll give me the original copies of the lady's statement, I'll block out her signature and try to convince him he should play ball with us or get his ass ready to go to prison. With this evidence we can have his federal probation revoked."

"You got it!" Richard exclaimed, and produced the statement for me.

"Okay, Richard, I know this is only one of the bastards you are concerned with. I'll maintain surveillance of Highways 21 and 115 in the hope of seeing Adkins in one of Ralph's cars. God only knows how long I'll have to watch. If he's making those trips, I'll guarantee you I'll keep at it until I see him. I'll keep in close touch with you."

Two days later I began one of the most boring ordeals of my career. Beginning at a spot on Highway 115 halfway between Charlotte and Statesville I eyeballed what seemed to be millions of cars every day, seven days a week. I usually worked twelve hours a day, constantly changing my location and working Highways 115, 16 and 21.

Finally in the middle of the third week at about 3:00 p.m. I spotted what I thought was the car described by the old lady Richard had arrested. Our theory was right. It was sandwiched in a bumper to bumper column of automobiles going south to Charlotte, evidently people going to work on the afternoon shift.

This was about fifteen miles north of Interstate 85, which accommodated both Charlotte and Gastonia. I estimated that within about an hour Adkins would have delivered the load of booze (if in fact he was making a delivery) and would again pass my position on 115, headed north to Wilkes County.

In about an hour and a half my vigil paid off! The Pontiac passed going north toward Wilkes County!

I followed him from a distance for about five miles. His speed was within the legal limits. Picking a good spot, I turned on my blue light and siren. As expected, he pulled over. This assured me that he had delivered his load.

I approached him on foot. ATF agents never used marked cars nor wore uniforms. Adkins appeared startled, seeing a federal agent rather than some county deputy looking for speeders.

"Hi, Don," I greeted him. "I see you are gainfully employed—you know, doing what the federal judge asked you to do. Remember I got him to give you probation and a suspended sentence instead of sending your ass to the pen.

"I won't ask you to open the trunk because I know you've already delivered Ralph's 20 cases or so. I'm not interested in a registration card for this car, because I'm sure it will be fictitious. That fact along with a few other things will be sufficient to get your probation revoked. Now, I've got an offer you can't afford to turn down."

"Joe, what the hell do you want with me? I thought we'd got rid of you. Some of us had a big party when you left. We'd rather see that goddamn government airplane flying over Wilkes than to see you back," he said.

"Don't worry about it, Don. I'm not moving back. I'm just in this part of the country to nail your boss, Ralph Shew. You're going to help do it or your ass is mud.

"My God, man! I ain't about to do that! He would sure as hell kill me. He's a mean son of a bitch. He would even kill you if he had half a chance and then piss on your grave," Adkins blurted. "I think you're bluffing. You ain't got nothing on me."

"Well, Don, one of our other agents has a case on you now. You are about to be indicted for delivering 150 gallons to one of Ralph's customers last month. You were driving this same car. We have pictures and sworn statements. The only hope in hell you have to avoid the five years facing you and at least another five years in the new case is to cooperate."

"How?" he asked.

"Well, first so you won't think I'm jerking you off, I'm going to let you see the original sworn statement of a number one witness." With that I let him see the statement except for the signature. He paled, then began perspiring profusely. I could see he was as nervous as a whore in church.

"Now all you have to do is provide us with information about Ralph's Wilkes County still, his stash place and when he is likely to be there. If we're successful in catching him we'll meet you someplace and let you see me burn the statements."

"Damn, the last thing I want to do is go to prison! But I don't want to be shot, either. If Ralph Shew ever even suspects me, I'm dead meat!" Adkins whined.

"Don, if you follow my instructions you won't have to worry about him suspecting you. If necessary we'll go to any limits to protect you. Just do what I tell you. That's better than going to prison, isn't it?"

"I'll need to think about it. I'll let you know in a few days."

I told him to meet me in two days at a certain Iredell County intersection at 10:00 p.m. I warned him that if he didn't show up we would immediately proceed with a new indictment and request a revocation of his current probation.

"You bastard," he said, "you aren't giving me a chance."

"Donald, you've had your quota of chances. Now I'll be there at the designated place. You be there, too."

At the appointed hour a car cruised into the intersection without lights. Undoubtedly it wasn't a liquor car. More likely it was an ordinary one. Looking in all directions, Adkins approached my government car. I asked him to sit in my car. "Are you ready to play ball?" I asked.

"It looks to me like I got no choice, but I'm telling you I don't like it. Am I going to get money for doing this?"

"I thought you would get to that. Yes, if we nail Shew I'll see that you get $1,000 cash."

"Now that's more like it, but I still don't like the deal. If I'm dead I sure as hell can't use the money."

"So, come fresh with the info," I said.

"Well, I ain't going to tell you about his other cars. Most of the other drivers are my friends and I ain't going to mess them up. That ain't going to bother you, though. Ralph has got a brand new 1965 Plymouth Satellite convertible with one of them Hemi souped-up engines. It's so hot that hell won't hold it. Now listen good. The feds, you know, them other SOB's like you, had a goddamn airplane up in Wilkes last week and blew up twenty-three shacks (a shack in that area is a moonshine still). Four of them belonged to Ralph, but he's got two more they didn't find and that's where he's getting his liquor. The one I'm talking about is on Cut-Throat Ridge. Do you know where that is?"

"I sure do," I replied. "I've spent a lot of time there in the past."

"Well, they's a real young married couple living there. The still is just over the ridge from this old house the couple lives in. They're just kids, maybe 18 or 20. The girl is a damn pretty little thing and stacked up like a brick shit house! I don't know where they come from, but I 'spect Ralph moved 'em in there.

"Now about this Hemi. Ralph will go to the house once't in a while in the Hemi. What I said while ago was, you'll not likely ever see him unless that Hemi comes there to load. If it does you can bet your sweet ass he'll be the driver. He ain't about to let anybody else get under the wheel unless it's Willie Clay Call, 'cause Willie Clay is one of the biggest and smartest bootleggers in the area. I really think that Willie is Ralph's backer. He paid for the Hemi! Ralph says he's a better driver than himself or even Junior Johnson.

"The still is supposed to run Thursday night. The young guy living there is one of the operators. When they run it he will haul the liquor down to the house, filter it and jar it up. This usually is done by the time the driver comes to haul it out, and it's most times not before midnight. I've been there a couple times with Ralph in that Hemi. Now I'm telling you, don't be stupid and try to catch him on the road, 'cause there ain't no way! The government ain't got a car or a driver that would have the chance of a snowball in hell. Since I'm doing this and putting my ass on the line I don't want you to fuck it up. If you do you won't get another chance and I'll be dead meat.

"If this don't work out—I mean, if they don't run the mash on Thursday they may be a little nervous about that government airplane. But I don't believe they'll move the still. Everybody knows the feds blowed up all the stills they found.

"There's a good chance Ralph will go to that stash 'cause that pretty little ole gal is fuckin' him. When I went there with him, the son of a bitch told her husband to get the hell out of the house for a while. He told me to watch the road, then he took her upstairs.

"One final thing: if you catch him don't turn your back on him for one minute 'cause he would just love to kill you. He told me so."

"Well, Don, where I come from, we kill each other," I replied.

I called Richard at 2:00 a.m. and reported my progress. After I filled him in he said, "Shit, all the action's going to be up in the Wilkes mountains, and me confined to my post."

"Well, buddy if it makes you feel better, remember that without your good work and unselfish cooperation we wouldn't have this opportunity to catch the big bad bastard," I replied.

My next move was to go to North Wilkesboro to make arrangements with the group supervisor for a crew to assist me. It was as cold as three feet up a polar bear's ass, probably about 15°F.

The leader of twelve rough and tumble agents gave me some bad news. They had located two monster stills and his total force was lying on those stills!

"The only agents on this post are Sam and myself. He's got a mean case of the flu," he stated.

"Well, my first desire is to check out the information. I can do that tonight if someone can drop me off. The real action should be tomorrow night," I informed him.

"I can do that but I can't provide you with a crew tonight; probably not tomorrow night either."

He was still using an old panel truck I had fixed up with a periscope and two-way radios when I was stationed at Wilkesboro. We used it many times for undercover work and for surreptitious entry into sensitive areas—*usually* without discovery.

At 1:00 a.m. that night he transported me to an area two ridges over from Cut-Throat. Having worked in the area I was able to negotiate the wilderness to get to the reported area, but my God! what a walk! It took me the better part of two hours to find what I was looking for. True to the information, I found the distillery with the mash ready for distillation! Several hundred yards west I saw the old mountain house where the young couple lived. There were no lights or other signs of life. The scene was perfect for such a nefarious enterprise as the manufacture and concealment of moonshine.

Silently and cautiously I retreated from the area and began the long and arduous trek to the spot where someone would pick me up. With my walkie-talkie radio I informed the pickup agent that I expected to be there no later than 5:00 a.m.

Our timing was excellent. On our return to Wilkesboro we discussed the negatives. First, the weather the following night would continue to be as cold as a well digger's ass in Alaska, meaning more equipment to lug across those near-vertical ridges. The second problem was finding enough agents to assist.

The latter contingency was the most serious. As to the first, we had no control over the weather. I have never known of anyone successfully suing God because of undesirable weather!

We wouldn't know how many if *any* agents would be available until we found out if they had completed either of the other investigations.

Upon returning to the ATF office, it didn't take long to find out via base radio that both crews were still making 24-hour surveillance and there would be no one available to assist in the raid.

A pow-wow with the group supervisor revealed that Sam, the oldest and most experienced agent at the post, had become sick and feverish and had to be evacuated from the surveillance area. Plans were that the supervisor would don his boots and raiding clothes, get off his executive ass and replace him.

"Well, that reduces this five man raiding crew down to one, me! No drop off driver means I'll have to walk a dozen miles and be lucky as hell to catch Rowdy Ralph. If I do catch him, from what I've heard about the bastard I'll be even luckier to hold him," I lamented.

"Well, Joe, Sam will feel good enough to drive you into the area, especially if you give him a swig of Jack Daniel's. That will still leave you to pull off the raid alone, and that makes the task much too dangerous. When Ralph Shew is involved it's damn dangerous even with half a dozen agents. You should call this off until later when we can furnish you some people."

"Bull shit. This sounds like the best shot we'll ever get at him. He has been hell on wheels for twenty years without being busted. I'm sure going to do my best to bust his ass tonight, with or without any help," I said.

"I'll call Sam and have him call you. Good luck and be careful."

It was near noontime so I went to the liquor store and purchased a fifth of J.D. I had some brunch and retired to my hotel room. I needed at least a couple of hours sleep before show time.

At about 5:00 p.m. Sam called. "The boss told me what you are going to do. I'm still sick but I can drive you into the area. I really can't help you with the raid, though. I have damn near had pneumonia. I think you are crazy to try to pull off a raid involving Ralph Shew all by yourself."

I replied, "I understand, Sam, but this seems to be the best opportunity we've had in years and I'm not about to pass it up. If you're sure you'll feel like dropping me off in the area, come by my hotel room about eight tonight. I'll treat us to a steak and we'll hold counsel with this jug of Jack Daniel's."

Sam was probably the best all-around ATF agent in the country when it came to experience competing with the violators in the Blue Ridge Mountains, especially in the Yadkin Valley county of Wilkes. He was the son of a sheriff in a mountain top county. Sam had a lovely country sense of humor and was as funny as a rubber crutch. He had been stationed in Wilkes County for many years and knew the territory as well as many people know their back yard. His ability had captured my immediate respect years before as a rookie assigned in the thick of things.

Sam arrived a little early. We wasted no time in consulting with Dr. J.D.

"I really appreciate this opportunity to socialize with you, Joe, since I'm the one who trained you in these mountains years ago. It was especially thoughtful of you to share your booze with me. You know how a wife is about liquor. I've got one of them Bible-totin' Baptist wives that are agin' it. She nags me into quittin' for a spell. To tell you the truth this is the first drink I've had in over three months. In those three months I ain't had a well day or a good time. That's probably the reason I got so sick laying on that still with all them young agents."

"Well, Sam, it looks like you're doing pretty good. Martha loves you and will try to take care of you."

"I don't know about that. She raises a lot of hell with me. She got a little cold on me in the bed for a while but I think things will get better. In fact, I almost got a piece last night—she had it with her," Sam confided.

"Sam, you have to understand this. The wife of any law enforcement officer doesn't have a pleasant road to travel. In ATF, it's even worse. The wife has our dinner on the table at 6:00 p.m. We don't make it. She throws out the dinner. For many succeeding days it's the same. They can accept that, but what they cannot accept is when we tell 'em there's no phones on those trees that we could use to call and explain."

After the bull session we went to a local club and knocked off a great steak. Sam drove me to within a mile of Cut-Throat Ridge in the old panel truck. He cautioned me about attempting a raid alone, especially one involving a bastard like Ralph Shew.

"It's the best we can do, Sam," I replied. "He's been operating far too long for us to pass up this opportunity."

I dropped out of the van about two ridges east of Cut-Throat, well equipped for an extended stay if necessary. Included in my pack was a goose down sleeping bag rated for zero weather, a fur lined jacket and the routine items such as flashlight, two way radio and still rations.

By midnight the temperature was no more than 15°F with winds at about 40 knots, making it as cold as an Eskimo's hemorrhoids.

Because of the extreme weather and the unavailable assistance of any other agents, I would have to do this all alone. It did seem like a stupid decision now, not waiting until later when I could easily get the eager assistance of many of the excellent agents assigned to North Wilkesboro. However, after many years of unsuccessful attempts by ATF to nail Ralph, my conscience wouldn't allow me to ignore my gut feeling of now or never.

I found the farm house where the alleged activities of filtering and loading the liquor were to take place, then settled down in a field some 200 yards from the house.

Any vehicle coming to the house would be immediately visible to me as it turned off the county road and down the long driveway.

I crawled into my sleeping bag with the Arctic coat on. I anticipated a very long wait for the appearance of bad ass Ralph. To my surprise, I had only been in position about 20 minutes when a vehicle turned down the drive toward the house.

The vehicle had to pass my position. I would be able to see it before it parked at the house. Holding my breath and crossing my fingers, I uttered a silent prayer, "Lord, let it be a Plymouth convertible!"

As the car passed me I could plainly see that it was just that! The Plymouth stopped near the house. The driver went inside.

Believing that the action was imminent, I crawled out of my toasty sleeping bag, tore off the warm coat and crawled up into the edge of the yard. There I could jump Ralph as he started loading the car.

I could hear voices inside. A few minutes later the young man of the house came out, got into the truck and drove away.

By now, without my coat, I was about to freeze. My gear was several hundred yards away in the field above the house. Afraid of being spotted if I tried to retrieve it, I decided to wait it out.

In about 30 minutes the pickup truck returned. The young man backed it up to the front porch and unloaded a 50 gallon steel barrel and a large cone-shaped felt object. We called these "felt hat" strainers. They were used to filter illegal liquor prior to pouring it into the containers.

The driver took the objects into the house unassisted. In all probability, according to what Adkins had told me, Ralph was occupied upstairs with the young lady doing stuff that comes naturally.

By this time it was about 2:00 a.m. For what seemed to be the better part of an Arctic winter, but really for about three hours, I damn near froze waiting on something to happen.

I realized that the bastards were filtering and proofing the liquor at their leisure! I crawled under the house, hoping to find the warm base of a chimney, but no such luck.

About 5:00 a.m. the men began bringing cases of liquor from the attic down to ground level.

Ralph Shew came out, started the powerful Hemi engine and backed the Plymouth up to the front porch. For a moment he sat under the steering wheel and revved up the engine. Leaving the engine idling, he got out and left the driver's side door open. This was obviously a routine precaution in case he needed to "get the hell out of Dodge."

Shew unlocked the trunk, raised the lid, reached into the door of the house and began bringing out cases of liquor. He carefully placed them into the trunk compartment.

I crawled as near to him as possible without alerting him, probably about 20 feet away. I hoped my half-frozen body could perform. I was going to need every ounce of strength I could muster.

Shew, six foot three and 200 pounds, was powerful and fast in his movements, violent and undoubtedly desperate. My greatest concern was to prevent him from getting into that awesome automobile.

After he loaded the sixth case of liquor and turned toward the stack to get another, I rushed him, cutting him off from access to the driver's side of the car.

Immediately he leaped away from me and off the porch. He ran into the darkness, throwing his handgun away. After chasing him about 100 yards I overtook him and made a flying tackle.

To my surprise, he offered no resistance.

Quickly, I arrested him and returned to the house and arrested the young couple. In searching Shew I found bullets for a 9 mm pistol. I asked him if he had thought about using the weapon on me. I considered his answer a compliment.

"Hell no, Joe! I know all about you. I'd be better off trying to sandpaper a cougar's ass than to take you on," he replied.

"Well, Ralph, from what I've heard about you, I'm damn glad you didn't." I responded by returning something like a compliment.

I contacted ATF in Wilkesboro on my walkie-talkie. Luckily one crew had given up on their surveillance and returned. Three volunteers were standing by to come to my assistance if needed.

They joined me and we destroyed the liquor and still, then took the prisoners in and stored the beautiful Hemi. Ralph Shew suggested that we let him drive it, since he was accustomed to it. After the loud laughter subsided I told Ralph we had no idea he had such a keen sense of humor.

Two nights later, Adkins and I met in another county and had an affidavit burning party. I paid him $1,000 cash.

Steamer still with homemade boilers fired by coke—typical of Ralph Shew's operation.

# KING OF THE
# MOONSHINERS

O ne could more accurately describe this chapter
of *Shortcuts to Justice* as a shortcut to *in*justice.

Deep in the heart of the Carolina tobacco country
existed a fifty year dynasty—an empire ruled by one
man.

This man was a legend during his lifetime and
thereafter. He was a very complex person, with superior intelligence and astounding generosity and courage. He was Joshua Percy Flowers.

Flowers owned and ruled over thousands of acres
of rich tobacco and timber lands, consisting of dozens
of tobacco farms tended by tenant farmers, or share-
croppers. Most of them were dependent upon him for
their livelihood.

His reputation was widespread. He was considered the King of the Moonshiners and was featured in
*The Saturday Evening Post,* complete with large cover
photograph, in 1958.

This is not an attempt to write his biography. I do not know enough of his early life—only about a few years in the 1960's. Even so, I can readily say that he was the most interesting and colorful person I have ever known.

In the early 1960's I was a special criminal investigator assigned to what I refer to as the racketeering squad of ATF, U.S. Treasury. I was given the responsibility of investigating Flowers.

From the time I joined ATF I heard of Flowers' reputation. At my initial briefing I learned that he was on the original list of 20 most important leaders of organized crime in the United States—a list created by U.S. Attorney General Robert F. Kennedy.

In researching volumes of files kept by federal agents including ATF, IRS and IRS Intelligence, I received quite an education. The federal government and the state of North Carolina had attempted for years to develop evidence to prosecute Flowers and a multitude of his alleged employees.

Although those who had tried to nail him were undoubtedly as competent as I (or more so), no one had developed a quality case in all those years.

There was a non-quality case tried against Flowers in federal court in the late fifties. Being stationed elsewhere, I only heard about this trial at the time, and read about it in the newspapers. The jury did not convict Flowers of the felonious crimes for which he was tried; instead he received a sentence of six months in prison for contempt of court.

It was some years later that I discovered, by coincidence, the shocking facts of that sentence. I will attempt to recount those facts later in this chapter and it will become evident why I have suggested that this should be an exception to the title *Shortcuts to Justice.*

Two senior ATF investigators, both very good at their work, had been investigating Flowers for years. Both had earned promotions and were transferred to other states. At that time the assignment fell to me.

I accepted it with mixed emotions. On the one hand, I considered the assignment an honor because only the best agents received such a mission.

On the other hand, after being briefed by the departing agents and reading over the files and monthly progress reports, it was obvious I would be playing in the big leagues. But what kid hasn't dreamed of playing in the big leagues?

With the support and assistance of many others, one being a disabled black veteran of World War II, I launched an all-out investigation.

The black veteran, Don Wiggins, was a man of great courage who was born and raised in the area owned by Flowers. He became disabled in combat during the Pacific Campaign.

Although Wiggins had known Flowers all his life, he never became involved in the liquor business. At this time Don was about 40 years old with a wife and several small children to support. His only income was a small pension from the Army.

During my briefing the departing agents had introduced me to Don. According to them, he had tried unsuccessfully to provide information on violations of the liquor laws.

The government paid rewards for valuable information. The quality of the information and the importance of the violator determined the amount of an award.

Don Wiggins had tried his best to report something of value but had never succeeded. Flowers' syndicate was flawlessly organized. Absolutely no one could gain access to the secrets of the whiskey empire except those deeply involved in the operation, and then only when so employed by Percy Flowers and personally approved by him.

Don had never sought employment with the Flowers syndicate. Consequently, although not trusted, he was never distrusted. When I heard this my mental light-bulb immediately switched on!

During my first secret meeting with Don, I laid out the blunt facts. The federal government wanted badly to develop a first-rate criminal case against Percy Flowers and would pay through the nose for the right kind of assistance.

This meant his working undercover to gain employment and the confidence of Percy Flowers.

To my surprise and delight he immediately agreed.

I met frequently with Don over the next several weeks, teaching him how to wear a hidden recorder and many other necessary techniques. He understood that if he succeeded he would have to testify in federal court.

Wiggins was an immediate success. Over a period of 18 months we developed a powerful conspiracy case including a multitude of substantive cases involving the syndicate's employees and co-conspirators.

Flowers was tried in the Wilmington division of the U.S. Eastern Judicial District of North Carolina in 1965.

Although Wilmington was selected because it was the farthest federal court location from Flowers' home area, we failed to obtain a conviction there. The jury was deadlocked and the judge declared a mistrial! We had enough evidence to convict the Pope!

This experience confirmed the legend that Percy Flowers could never be convicted by a jury in North Carolina.

My experiences investigating the Flowers syndicate left me with the feeling that I had become acquainted with one of the most complicated and interesting individuals in the world—a fearless, violent individual characterized by extreme generosity who was greatly feared by some, admired by some and respected by all.

Upon entering the service of any government law enforcement agency in those days, one would invariably hear of the notorious J. Percy Flowers, the King of the Moonshiners. Never would an agent be told what I learned through my experience in tracking him for years—there was another side that was a real paradox.

Flowers was married, for life, to a good lady who was respected by all. I have never heard a negative comment about her from anyone with whom I came in contact—only praise for her character, good neighborliness and family values.

They had two children: the older was a son; the younger, a daughter named Rebecca. It was common knowledge that Flowers would not involve any family member in his illegal enterprise under any circumstances.

Part of the legend of J. Percy Flowers was that his only son grew up with good values, totally sheltered from any illegal activities. He graduated from the University of North Carolina and entered its law school. Tragically, he was killed when his private airplane crashed on the way home to Johnston County from Chapel Hill.

Percy's only remaining child, Rebecca, was still a small child when I retired from ATF. It is my understanding that she is now married and the mother of twin boys. She owns and operates the family farms and a large retail store offering a wide variety of merchandise, among other interests. She is well educated and respected, an asset to the community—a brilliant business executive who obviously inherited her mother's character and her father's intelligence.

I was a United States Army Reserve major when this assignment was laid on me and was acquainted with a Regular Army major who was an advisor to my reserve unit in Raleigh. That major owned a cabin on the inland waterway in Brunswick County, N.C. It was adjacent to a cabin (more like a mansion) owned by Percy Flowers. My major told me the following story.

An 18 year old kid was playing around on the waterway with a brand new 18 foot fiberglass inboard motorboat. The inland waterway is influenced by the ocean tide and on this occasion the tide was low.

The major was standing on the shore talking to his neighbor, Percy Flowers, when the young man hit a stump and ripped a hole in the bow of his new boat. Neither of them knew the young man, who got out of his boat and loudly wept!

Flowers walked down to the water's edge. "Bad luck, son," he said. "How much will it cost to repair your boat?"

In tears, the young man said, "My daddy will kill me. He helped me borrow the money to buy this boat. It'll probably cost twelve or fifteen hundred dollars to fix it!"

Without another word, Flowers pulled a large roll of bills from his pocket, counted off fifteen one-hundred dollar bills and handed them to the boy. He probably would never see him again!

When asked for a contribution by church members who wanted to build a new church, Flowers responded: "Build your church and send me all the bills." He paid for the church in its entirety.

On another occasion, an out-of-state traveling salesman was entertained with a flat tire about a mile from Flowers' store. He did not have a spare tire or the equipment for repair. He walked to Flowers' store and told him about his problem. Flowers took a new tire from his stock, drove the salesman back to his car, and helped him install the new tire—FOR FREE—no charge whatsoever! The salesman did not even know him.

There were many similar stories about the man.

He was well established socially, having some of the most prominent and influential politicians in the state as friends.

He was the state's most famous breeder of fox hounds, with hundreds of acres of land fenced primarily for his multitude of dogs. They constantly won blue ribbons at field trials.

His competitive spirit was obvious in other places as well. He was active in breeding, training and fighting game cocks. According to many local citizens, he actually built a large concrete arena to feature cock fights in arrogant disregard of North Carolina state law. No state or county law enforcement officers ever challenged his cock fighting.

One story has it that Flowers went to a place in Texas where gambling and cock fighting were open and popular. His prize rooster lost to a Texas rooster in an annual cock-fighting event, which allegedly cost Percy $50,000. The rumor (which I believe) says that he thanked the winners without a hint of resentment or disappointment. "I'll see you folks next year," was his only comment.

Always a winner, Percy imported to Johnston County a citizen of Puerto Rico who was an expert in breeding game cocks, to breed a rooster that could defeat anything in Texas.

The expert lived for free with his wife and children on one of Flowers' many farms. No one knows what he was paid.

Jose was ready by the time the next Texas tournament rolled around. The prize rooster remained a secret. Flowers revealed none of his plans, even to his family.

Jose and Percy drove to Texas and entered the special hi-tech rooster in the tournament.

Having great confidence in Jose and his prize rooster, Percy bet $100,000 on the outcome. The bets were enormous because this was the so-called big league where the very wealthy chose to bet on their roosters!

When the arena manager called for the fight against Flowers' rooster, he announced that the match would between the Texas champion and a former loser from North Carolina, name unknown.

The experts gave four-to-one odds that the Texas champion would win.

No one knows how many of these side bets Flowers challenged. People with him said he was totally confident in his rooster's ability to win.

The big cock fight was the grand finale of the tournament.

It was not even interesting. Percy Flowers' unknown rooster mutilated the Texas champion in four minutes—fatally!

No one knows how much money Percy Flowers won and it really is not important. He deserved whatever it was!

These stories challenge one to look at the man in different ways. He probably viewed the laws of the

United States as running counter to the forms of justice that he honored, unlike those who said, "Well, it's the law."

They have to mean something to those of us who received training and admonishment that Percy Flowers was a racketeer who had to bite the dust.

Percy Flowers, from the viewpoint of an investigator, was a target. "Get him!" the bosses demanded.

There was a problem, however. No one had ever gotten him. This is what I was facing.

I had negative feelings for a long time after the hung jury that tried Flowers in 1965. We provided dynamite evidence against him that should have convicted anyone. The enormous power of his personality, his political influence, his wealth, his Robin Hood reputation, and the fear he instilled in many who knew him, prevailed.

As far as I was concerned he made a liar out of the poet who created the not-so-immortal adage, "crime does not pay!"

In retrospect I have to acknowledge admiration and respect for him— not approval or respect for his criminal activities of course, but for his intelligence and strength.

Long before my appearance on the scene in eastern North Carolina, the federal government had dispatched crack agents of the IRS and ATF to investigate Flowers for income tax evasion as well as his involvement in the illegal whiskey business.

After a joint effort by the state and federal governments, the state brought a multitude of misdemeanor charges against him in 1958—for example, false registration of vehicles. The federal agents had some evidence of undercover purchases of nontaxpaid whiskey from hirelings of Flowers.

As Flowers was considered a national figure, the chief of ATF enforcement in Washington dispatched one of his favorite undercover black agents to Raleigh to assist in a follow-up purchase from Flowers, or actually from one of his flunkies. A political appointee and former military officer, the chief was deeply involved in promoting his special undercover squad, constantly searching for glory for them and having a real hard-on for anyone in the South, not only the violators but also the agents.

Almost any good undercover agent could make purchases of illegal liquor from people believed to be hirelings of Flowers—no big deal! *No one* could connect them to Flowers, however! The agent received instructions to go to Raleigh, N.C. and accompany the undercover agent in making an additional purchase from the Flowers syndicate to strengthen the case and corroborate the other agent's story.

In my opinion the truth is the idiot who was the chief of ATF at the time wanted the glory of making a case against Flowers solely to justify to Congress his black undercover team. No officer had ever made a direct purchase from Percy Flowers and neither did this black SOB! He did accompany an undercover agent and participate in a purchase of illegal whiskey from one of Flowers' many alleged minor employees.

When Flowers cursed the black agent in open court, he received a six-month sentence for contempt.

I did not know until some time later that the black agent from Washington was *the same* agent whom Washington had sent some years before to another city where I was stationed. He was to accompany a professional civilian informant, to corroborate the testimony of the informant in that area. His instructions were to use U.S. government funds to purchase illicit whiskey with the help of the professional informant, to destroy the whiskey and make an affidavit to that effect and to testify to that evidence. No deviation from that policy was allowed.

The informant, who was a special employee of ATF and paid with government funds, enjoyed the reputation in many southern states of having engineered hundreds of quality cases. After only two days, the special employee reported to me that the federal ATF agent sent to assist him had propositioned him to help resell the contraband purchased from the violators—a felony!

The special employee warned him against such an act and reminded him that they had to sign sworn statements that they had destroyed the illicit whiskey purchased with government funds. According to the special employee, the agent resold the whiskey anyway, pocketing the proceeds, then made affidavits that the contraband had indeed been destroyed!

I reported this to my supervisor immediately and requested that he allow me to pursue a criminal indictment against this traitor.

"Hell no, Joe, put that black son of a bitch on the next plane to Washington, D.C. and keep your mouth shut about it!"

I was already up to my ass in problems at that post so I did as he suggested. I fully expected to hear that the crooked bastard had soon been fired. But I never heard any more—until two or three years later.

At that time the mental midget ex-army colonel who was our national chief and the father of the so-called special squad came to Raleigh for a conference with all ATF personnel in North Carolina. That conference included my boss, several supervisors and about seventy of my peers.

During this period, those of us charged with doing the difficult job of eradicating the moonshine business were unhappy—more specifically described as pissed off—with the Washington, D.C. bureaucrats for being obstructive. They would not issue us FM radios, which other agencies such as the FBI, DEA, Customs and even local police departments had been using for years. Instead, we still limped along with the old AM type—to make matters worse they were a bastard brand manufactured in the California home town of our chief.

By the time of the conference, the chief had suffered so many complaints from field personnel that he was sensitive to the subject, but still seeking support from the field.

"Ah!" said the chief. "You men are in the heart of illicit whiskey manufacturing country. Surely you use our radio system for the urgent communications necessary to accomplish your mission. Now! I would like to ask you if you can give me an example of a good use you have made recently of your walkie-talkie radios!"

Most hard working agents, though thoroughly disgusted with the situation, were understandably reluctant to comment to this big shot whom most had never even seen in person.

Not big mouth Joe. "Yes, sir," I announced. "I recently used a walkie-talkie to great advantage!"

"Fine, fine. Now gentlemen, Carter is known in Washington as an exceptional agent. Please listen to his remarks. I'm sure you'll agree with him."

I stood up and said, "Well, Chief, I was on foot, well up the side of White Head Mountain."

"Yes, yes, go on and tell us just what you used the walkie-talkie for!"

"Yes, sir, I killed a goddamn rattlesnake with it," I explained. I sat down.

"Boy! you have just shit in your mess kit!" whispered a co-hort seated next to me.

"I want to talk to you, and bring that rebel with you, as soon as this meeting is over," said the chief to my supervisor.

When the meeting ended, my supervisor, one of the best men I have ever known, came to me in private.

"Joe, you may have been too forward and that jerk will raise hell with both of us, but you gave him a message he needed to hear. Rough but real I'm with you. Don't worry too much—our orders come from the regional office in Atlanta. Just take it easy when he talks to us."

We met with the chief in my private office. He was in a rage. "This agent must be a mental case," he stormed. "He crashes into areas where angels fear to tread! Carter, I'm going to give you a chance to apologize for your disrespectful comment at the conference. Now, what do you have to say?"

"Chief, any agent in the field attempting to use your radios will tell you the same thing. We can easily hear the weather ships on the Mediterranean Sea but cannot hear the poor bastard down in the woods who's trying to communicate with us."

"Anything else?" the chief asked.

"Yes, sir, what about the black agent I caught up in Elizabeth City about three years ago, reselling illicit whiskey purchased with government funds and swearing it had been destroyed? I have not heard of him being prosecuted as I recommended, let alone being fired."

"Apparently you do not realize that Investigator X was the witness who only recently sent your untouchable criminal, the King of the Moonshiners Percy Flowers, to prison when none of your southern redneck agents could do it!" The chief was adamant.

*This was a real shock.* I knew nothing of that trial except what I had read in the papers. Flowers had served a six-month sentence for contempt for calling the agent a "lying son of a bitch." Now I agree with Flowers. He really was a lying SOB! But too late to say so!

I'm sure that neither the judge, the district attorney, the defense attorneys, the agents, nor I knew that this corrupt agent was the same one at the time of the 1958 trial. Flowers was acquitted of all charges in the indictment. It was only the contempt charge that brought about his prison sentence—a travesty of justice and a shortcut to *injustice* by the government.

This revelation by the so-called chief of enforcement of the national office in Washington hit me like a ton of bricks. This SOB was apparently the only federal official who had an inkling of the use of a corrupt agent in a criminal trial, *knowing* I had nailed the corrupt agent years before. It was mind boggling. I suppose the gravity of this scandal caused me to make a further statement, unheard of from an agent in the field to the big man in Washington.

"Chief, this is sad. The six-month sentence has already been served. The only thing left for me to say is, if that agent SOB is still on the job, I will contact my congressman and report this."

With that, I walked out, contemplating the possibility of seeking a new job.

That did not become necessary. Soon afterward, I heard that the crooked agent was given the opportunity to resign, *but* he was never prosecuted.

It seems that for decades the only way the federal government could bring about any degree of punishment to Percy Flowers was by an act of *in*justice—a six month prison sentence for contempt of court for cursing the black undercover ATF agent.

Under the circumstances, the federal judge did exactly right. The U.S. Attorney for the eastern district did his duty by using the agent as a witness. The ATF supervisors did the right thing in recommending the case for prosecution. *None* of them knew at the time that the agent was corrupt—an individual who was exactly what Percy Flowers called him in open court, namely, "A goddamn lying son of a bitch."

I will always feel bad about this for two reasons. First, because my agency never agreed to prosecute him. Not only that, it did not until years later fire him from the job. Instead, some creep in Washington covered the whole thing up, and of all things, dispatched him to get Percy Flowers.

The war between the hunter (law enforcement officers) and the hunted (violators of the law) is a single-edged sword. The criminal follows no rules, only the natural law of self-preservation.

Officers of the law are supposedly bound by honor, law, policy and many other restraints. Therefore it is an unfair match.

To compound the problem, youngsters now entering law enforcement as a career usually have an education. In that training they hear more of what they cannot do than what they can.

The sob-sisters and liberal bleeding hearts such as the ACLU and federal court of appeals judges who are always ruling on points of law to benefit the convicted criminal, with no concern for the victim, intimidate the young people who wear a badge. The adverse effect is that most of them are afraid to go to extremes to solve a crime.

Even in my day we would never frame a defendant or exaggerate a case such as was done in the trial of Percy Flowers in 1958.

In summary I will offer some comments on the man. I realize that if I were still in the service, these remarks would get me either fired or transferred far away. So be it!

Flowers was on an organized crime list of the 20 most wanted criminals in the U.S.

The Internal Revenue Service had agents assigned to get Flowers for years—probably from 1950 forward. None succeeded!

ATF had agents assigned to investigate Flowers' involvement in the illegal whiskey business, from about 1940 to 1970. He was never convicted in any major case.

Flowers was a multi-millionaire who owned 7,000 acres of rich tobacco and timber land. He supported 23 families who lived on his land. Some of them worked in his whiskey operation. Many did not. He supported them anyway.

There are many more stories about the man, both pro and con. Anyone who evaluates these stories will come up with the opinion either that Percy Flowers was a vicious, corrupt major criminal *or* that he was a compassionate, generous person who only defied the law when he felt the law was wrong.

My own analysis is that Percy Flowers was a better version of Robin Hood, an honorable family man, a brilliant and resourceful individual. He was a man who lived by his own laws and who had no respect for social laws if they conflicted with his agenda. Thousands of people admired him for his strength. He was a man whom the U.S. government could never get twelve persons on a jury to convict.

During my career in ATF, I never failed to bring to justice any major violator I was assigned except J. Percy Flowers.

Because of his priority status with the U.S. government as a desirable target, I used all of my talent and resources to nail Flowers. I lost!

It was not because we had no evidence, nor because we didn't try.

The truth is, we lost because Flowers flat beat us. His image and influence overwhelmed all the energy and effort the U.S. government could muster.

After writing my first book, *Damn the Allegators*, I received many orders through the mail. Several included letters commenting favorably about Flowers, whom I called "Paul Barker." I believe he had thousands of admirers.

The things I learned about him during my investigation have convinced me he was very intelligent, a born leader, a good family person and one who stood head and shoulders above many who criticized him. He was strong, and woe be it unto anyone who got too much in his way. He was a man whose crimes only involved dealing in illegal whiskey—crimes considered commercial crimes, not crimes of violence.

In the final analysis, I will say this:

He had the potential to be successful in any number of endeavors.

The thought strongest in my mind is that he would have made a great military general in any of our great wars, especially the War Between the States.

In my opinion he will be remembered more fondly than any governor North Carolina has ever had.

Alamance County, N.C. steamer still. Note "Still Buggy" on right - used in woods to work distilleries.

# BLAST AND RUN

The following story was originally published in *Damn the Allegators*. It is included in this book because it is an ideal example of "Shortcuts to Justice."

The rifle shot cracked with a shattering *sqpw-yaeeee*. I dropped to the ground and hugged it like mad. Only Reb Estes could have fired that shot on this farm. He owned it through title to a relative, a common practice. We had never seen nor could we prove that he tried to shoot federal agents searching for his moonshine stills, but we knew it to be a fact.

I could see no trace of the trigger man. The shot, like so many others in the past, came from hiding. With drawn revolver I looked for a target, knowing I would find none.

All law enforcement people called Reb evil, mean and vicious. Folks said the devil grabbed Reb from his mother's womb and commissioned him to the life of crime. He had killed several men in the past, but never had he been convicted. He was a giant in the Carolina liquor business, also being connected with an interstate auto theft ring. The North Carolina State Bureau of Investigation constantly sought him, but like us, they were never quite successful in building an airtight case on him.

Two or three more shots zinged by but none as close as the first. I lay in a ditch, relatively safe for several minutes, my eyes searching for his presence. I had told the boys that the best thing we could do was to catch him at an opportune moment and kill him. But he never allowed us this opportunity.

It must have been an hour before I dared move on with my search. No more rifle shots were heard. I continued the routine search for his distillery with no luck.

"Damn him," I thought. "I'm getting a bellyful of his shooting sprees. I'm gonna get even with that bastard. He's gonna pay. How can we fix him? Not necessarily bodily harm, but what can we do to let him know we won't tolerate his actions?"

By the time I got back to my pickup rendezvous, I had decided to organize a midnight raiding party. Tonight, I knew where he kept several cars concealed. Most being used in the liquor business and probably some of them stolen and repainted. I didn't mention my plan to the agent who picked me up because he was young and I didn't want to subject him to the type of deal I was planning. Besides, I didn't know him well enough to trust him.

Back at ATF headquarters, I consulted Grandy, who had had plenty of trouble with Reb. "Sure, shoot the sonofabitch if you can get away with it," he advised. "But I can't go with you tonight. I've got other work to do."

Later in the day I ran into Mack, a good agent friend who worked in Reb's territory, anyway. He was delighted. "I'm sure as hell glad to find someone willing to do something to the bastard," he raved. Mack volunteered to recruit several local officers who hated Reb and were willing to go with us.

To damage him financially was sufficient to satisfy my irritation with him at this time. But in such a night raid, which would be done as vigilantes and not as an official law enforcement act, special talent would be required. Too, when you get close, you never know just what will happen. Maybe we would get that chance to kill him, a real stroke of luck. That is, if we could get by on justifiable homicide.

I cautioned Mack about the state officer personnel he recruited for this mission. They had to be completely reliable and capable of **"DENYING THE ALLEGATIONS AND DAMNING THE ALLEGATORS"** in the event anything went wrong. Mack was very sure of two state agents. I knew them both and concurred. We had worked together for quite a while and all of us knew too much on each other already which precluded forever any mention of this unauthorized, clandestine, retaliatory act we were about to commit.

Mack and I raided all the government cars we could find and borrowed all the dynamite, detonators and fuse we could muster. We also took along a good supply of ammunition.

We met Hal and Dave in the edge of the city and held a brief council of war. I laid it out. "The sonofabitch took a few more shots at me today," I told them and watched it soak in.

Hal said, "That makes me mad as hell; he's done the same to me twice, and he's too yellow to let you see him when he does it."

This was easy, working these men into the fury necessary to motivate them into helping me do what I had planned. For a while, I thought I had overdone it, as they were primed to go too far. I explained that I didn't want anyone hurt, rather that our mission was to destroy his fleet of liquor cars. Quickly I described their hiding place.

Then we set out with blood in our eyes, each hoping that some way, Reb would get in the way and give us an excuse to shoot him. "Too much to hope for," I thought.

We pulled into a familiar hiding place in the woods along the highway, about halfway to our destination, to wait for later hours and to swig on the bottle I'd brought along. After two or three drinks each, we were even thirstier for Reb's blood. Someone retold the old story about Reb cursing the Lord when it rained hard and during thunderstorms. He is alleged to have said that when he died, instead of going to heaven, he hoped to go to a place where there was nothing but one big whiskey still.

At midnight we departed to complete the infamous journey. Around 1:00 a.m. we reconnoitered at the hiding place of the whiskey cars. They were locked behind a rickety gate and fence complex which once had been somebody's dream of another Darlington 500. This long abandoned country racetrack gave Reb an excellent place to hide fifteen or twenty whiskey cars, along with a couple of large trucks for distant transportation of the booze.

As we glided by for a second look, I jumped out of the slowly moving car and checked the lock on the gate. It had to go. We could not afford the encumbrance of climbing over the fence, doing our dirty work, then re-scaling the fence. That obstacle could turn into a dangerous trap. The lock was a No. 7 Masters, very difficult to pick, especially in the darkness. A better idea, I thought, was to dynamite it.

I gave the radio signal and the car rolled up to me in the darkness and I got in. "Go down the road a short distance," I told Mack, who stopped in a spot shielded by trees. "Unlock the trunk. We need about three sticks of dynamite." He prepared the charge. "Now we need a double for each car and truck. The last time I climbed that fence, there were a good dozen, so let's fix twelve double charges."

In thirty minutes the lethal charges were complete, each armed with a cap and fuse.

"We'll have to act fast after we blow the gate. I'll jump out and take care of that. Mack, you go back up the road and I'll call you on the radio as soon as the charge is ignited. It has a forty-second fuse, so be close by and smash through the opening as soon as the blast is over. Pick me up at the gate. We'll have a short ride to the vehicles. Mack, you keep the motor running and watch for the approach of anyone. We'll tape the charges to the gas tanks of each vehicle that we can get to."

This would have to be done instantly, as the proper way to use dynamite in multiples is to split the ends of each fuse, ignite one, and spray the ends of the group. This always ignites the others as the sparks spray shoots into the open split, hitting the live powder in the fuse. However, once activated the stuff goes rapidly, so all hands must clear out.

Loaded with bombs, the government car passed back by the gate and again I dropped off into the darkness with three sticks of dynamite for a gate lock that had to go.

I eased up to the gate and taped the charge midway between the two hinges on the anchor post. This blast would make toothpicks out of the wood in the gate. But who might hear the blast and come running?

I was confident of our schedule though. We should complete the whole operation in two minutes plus. We did not have to wait for the blast once the charges had been placed on the vehicles. In fact, I deemed it highly inadvisable to wait, even though this was a sparsely settled community.

With a steady hand, I ignited the charge fuse and gave Mack the radio signal.

Forty seconds later, a tremendous blast obliterated the gate, its anchor post, and two or three spans of fencing on that side. Before the smoke had settled, Mack appeared with the car door open. I jumped in and someone handed me four double charges with the fuses already split. In a few more seconds, we covered the short distance to where the beautiful hot rods were parked.

"Damn,' I thought, "We'll give ole evil Reb some-thing to remember." I knew at a sweeping glance the total value of the vehicles would approximate $100,000.

Like a backfield in a huddle, we quickly ignited the dynamite, using the leap frog system, that is, plac-ing of the first in line, another man the second, another the third. When the first man finished taping his charge he would place his second charge on vehicle number four and so on. The taping and ignition took only one and one-quarter minutes. Quickly we jumped in the car from which we had removed the license plate and substituted one of a dozen from many different states that each ATF car normally car-ries, and we prepared to flee. "Not yet, Mack, we've got a few seconds, circle the pool." Mack dug up dirt circling the cars. With .38 drawn, I proceeded in. Then we cleared the opening and headed north just as the explosions began.

There is a distinct difference in the beauty of an explosion made on a commonplace object compared to that made when fuel is involved. The dynamite set off the gas tanks and the sight of each was something to behold—huge orange towers of flame shooting into the night like major fuel dump fires.

There had been sixteen cars, but the terrible dev-astation we had meted out to the twelve, undoubtedly blew up the remainder, including the two-ton silver van truck parked in the middle.

"That'll teach the bastard to shoot at an officer of the law." Mack muttered.

Dave said he knew of a barn, stacked full of whiskey jars, that he thought belonged to Reb. "Why not just let's go on now and bum the barn?"

"Nope," I said. "We won't push our luck too far tonight. But if that son of a bitch ever shoots at one of us again, we'll really fix him the next time."

We pulled silently and without lights into a woods road about a mile away. The whole horizon glowed red from the fire. I was thankful that the cars were in the center of the old race track where the fire could not spread to the woods and possibly from there to some innocent person's property.

# WEEKEND WARRIOR

**O**nce in a great while I would interrupt the ATF adventure by playing soldier as a military police officer in the U.S. Army Reserve. On one memorable occasion I grabbed a fifteen-day tour at Fort Bragg, N.C. as a Military Police Captain, a "weekend warrior".

I had a good friend there, Lt. Col. Raymond LeVann, who was the commanding officer of the famous 503rd MP Battalion. I had served with him on many previous occasions. He was a much-decorated veteran of WW II and the Korean war.

On this occasion Col. LeVann said that my arrival was an excellent reason for a party in conjunction with another celebration which was to transpire at the 82d Airborne Division Officers Club that night, a big gathering of the Army Chaplains, mostly Catholic. "Sounds great Ray, but we won't be able to drink, will we, since they are all ministers?"

Ray laughed, "Hey, remember, I told you they were all Catholic, like me! Hell, the only time they put water in their mouth is to brush their teeth."

And what a party! Those holy people wheeled the booze out in wheelbarrows! This was a new experience for me! Drunk preachers. And me, coming from a culture of Southern Baptists, who were more critical of anyone who used alcohol than they were of serial rapists.

For the few hours remaining of the night after the party at Ray's home, he entertained me with many of his war stories until he fell asleep. Shortly thereafter he woke me and asked how I felt. "Lousy," I told him. He said, "Me too, I've got the damnedest hangover since Christmas. Do me a favor, will you. Open my back door and let my cat in so I can kiss his ass to get this bad taste out of my mouth!"

As Ray was a good Catholic, I couldn't resist telling a humorous story one of the Chaplains told me.

Two southern rednecks went across the country to see the Super Bowl, from their reserved seats near the fifty-yard line. Just before kickoff time two Catholic Nuns sat down directly in front of them, completely blocking their view of the field. They were wearing the type of headwear bonnets that Nuns must wear. "Look at that. This is a hell of a note. We spend all our money getting here and paying for the tickets, and them Catholic nuns block our view. I wish we were somewhere else."

The other guy said, "Yeah, I wish we were where was no Catholics."

One of the Nuns turned and softly said, "Why don't you go to hell, mister, there are no Catholics there."

Up at 6:00 AM. clean shaven and immaculate in a class "A" uniform, and sharp as a tack, with no indication of having drunk a barrel of booze the previous night, Ray woke me and informed me of my assignment. I was to work with two Army criminal investigators on a mission to apprehend two young Army deserters who had overpowered a stockade guard, robbing him of his wallet and two weapons—a 12 gauge riot shotgun loaded with double ought buckshot, and a forty five caliber automatic pistol. They were last seen running into the woods across the road from the stockade.

Later in the morning I joined the agents, both of whom were dressed in civilian business suits with no indication of rank.

Fort Bragg, N.C. is one of the largest military reservations in the United States, having thousands of acres of ranges and woodlands. Countless trails and dirt roads and man made lakes are found throughout. Our mission to capture the escapees involved driving over these trails in what I call a speculative search. Late in the afternoon while deep in this wilderness, I noticed an automobile parked at the side of a small lake about 200 yards from our position. There was a clearing from the road and the lake, probably a parking lot for vehicles of service men and their families on picnic outings.

I told the driver to stop the car, that I thought I had seen someone lying behind the parked car. Immediately, the driver stopped, grabbed a carbine and jumped behind a large tree. The other agent with his carbine quickly crouched behind an embankment, just as they were trained to do. The fugitive bastards holding the riot gun and the .45 covered the open area between themselves and us! A BIG problem.

Armed only with my little "airweight" Colt .38 revolver, like a damn fool I walked the distance of the clearing to the car. When I eased around the front of the car, I was looking right down the bore of the deadly .45, and much worse, the shotgun. I looked squarely in the faces of two desperate and evil looking punks. With the hammer back, I pointed my little insignificant revolver at the left eye of the one with the shotgun. My comment to them was automatic and sounded strange, even to me. "If you son of a bitches don't throw down those weapons this place is going to be littered with blood and guts is just a few seconds." Staring him in the eyes, I slowly tightened my finger on the trigger. Just in time the barrel of the shotgun dropped toward the ground. Then, both threw their weapons on the ground.

The two agents ran up and put shackles on the fugitives.

The former shotgun bearer, apparently the leader of the two, snarled at me, "You crazy '90 day wonder!' Son of a bitch I'll guarantee you that if those other bastards had come strolling across that clearing like a bunch of kids out for school recess like you just did, all of you would be dead now. But I knew if I shot you those SOB's would get us with those goddam machine guns they're carrying."

I was wearing a class 'A' Army Captain's uniform and insignia, and told him, "Watch your step, soldier, you're talking to a commissioned officer of the U.S. Army."

"Fuck you, you dumb shit, you take me to that old bastard general with the four stars, and I'll cuss him out, too."

After returning the prisoners to the stockade, we went by the EM club and consumed enough 'happy hour' beverages to calm the nerves of an alligator. In a respectful way, agent Morris scolded me. "With all due respect sir, I've never seen anyone do what you did today. All I can say is that either you have more guts than anyone I have ever known, or else you are the most stupid and reckless. Would you believe that we would have called for a 100 man SWAT team to capture those guys!"

"You are at least half right Mr. Morris, I admit that what I did was nuts, but to tell you the truth, I didn't take this mission seriously enough. I just assumed that those guys were a couple of kids who wanted to go home for Christmas." I found out later that they had robbed a couple service stations and were suspected of one or more murders.

The next morning agents Morris and Cole were waiting for me at the office of Col. LeVann. "Good news Captain Carter, the Provost Marshal of the whole post is waiting for us to bring you to headquarters, he's going to honor us with some special award ceremony for courage in apprehending the escapees."

"You guys go ahead and take the honor, I'll stay out of it. After all I'm a civilian and won't be here much longer." What I did was reckless and I had probably violated every rule in the manual. I didn't need the Provost Marshal or the commanding General to tell me that. I already knew it.

# THE BLACK PREACHER FROM VIRGINIA

He gently pecked on the door to the U.S. Treasury Department's ATF office in Raleigh, North Carolina.

He was immaculately dressed in a double-breasted $400 Italian silk navy blue suit, black patent leather shoes, a white silk tuxedo shirt complete with ruffles, diamonds in his lapel and on most of his fingers. The huge black man, a sight to behold, entered on invitation by agent Bill Walden. Walden introduced himself and asked if he could be of assistance. The impressive stranger replied, "I's rather convinced you can, but I can be of much more assistance to you and the federal guv'ment than you can be to me. I is the Reverend Samuel P. Warlock from Virginia. I covers the flock at Bethel Baptist Church near Richmond."

"And in what way, sir, can you be of service to us?" Walden asked.

"Well, you see, I is willing to be your ace undercover operator. I can purchase evil spirits from any man, woman or child regardless of their color—be it black, white, red, yellow or polka dot. I is willing to undertake such a dangerous mission out of love for my country but especially out of my greater love for Almighty God—depending, of course, on the size of the rewards on the bootleggin' bastards' heads," explained Rev. Warlock.

"In other words Preacher, your unrestricted love for God and country is measured in terms of dollars?"

"Mr. Walden, that is, Agent Walden, you is so right. You see, bruthah, it takes many dollahs to carry on the holy work of the Lawd. But I is sure our guv'ment is amply equipped with sufficient money to courageously pursue this important task. Is I right?"

"Well, the government has special funds for the purchase of evidence, but unfortunately those funds are only for use against our biggest violators. It's doubtful that you can deal directly with them," Walden replied.

"I don't know any of them but I will guarantee you I can buy moonshine from anyone. I could buy whiskey from Mother Teresa, believe it or not!"

With that Agent Walden invited the reverend into my office next door, explaining that I was assigned to work on major cases and could easily get the funds.

As Walden escorted this fabulous creature into my office and began relaying his claims to me, I was thinking about the previous week. Percy Flowers had beaten the U.S. government and me in a major federal court trial.

I turned my attention to the preacher and listened intently. Maybe, just maybe this so-called minister of the gospel would be another way to get at Percy.

I questioned Rev. Warlock. "Have you had experience in undercover work?"

"Mr. Cartah, I has a world of experience in encouraging people to do what I ask them," the preacher replied.

"Rev. Warlock, this is serious and dangerous work we are doing. If in the unlikely event you are able to make a direct purchase of illegal alcohol from our major violators such as Douglas Ross or Percy Flowers, you would be required to testify against them in federal court," I cautioned.

"I fully understands that—trust me, that will be no problem."

The man was so confident in his abilities that we decided to try him. Walden was caught up in the preacher's enthusiasm, which was normal for him.

"Well, Preacher, is there a car you can use?" I asked.

"Oh, yes! I's got a brand new gold 98 Oldsmobile! I will use that!"

"We'll pay you for the use of your car and provide you with money to purchase the illicit whiskey. You will be closely monitored, so don't try to fuck us up about the federal money—understand?"

"Oh, Mr. Cartah, don't you worry about that. I is a minister of the gospel. I will be straight with you boys!" he assured us.

"Okay. We'll need to be in contact with you almost daily. Look out this window. Do you see that 7-Eleven store parking lot across the street? We'll meet over there in the parking lot."

"Well, Mr. Cartah, that particular place just won't do. You see that First Citizens Bank branch next to it? This 98 I'm driving was financed there and I hasn't got around to making any payments on it. Frankly, they's looking for my car!"

"Okay, here's my home telephone number. Call me when you make a contact. Do you need a place to live?"

"Don't worry about that, Mr. Cartah. I's got a real good place to live. You see, I has been traveling around the rural area and has become acquainted with some Christian sistahs up in Franklin County. They wants me to live at their place at no cost. I told them I was a man of God in need of a building to hold services—in other words, a church. So they run the chickens out of a chicken house and let me use that. Now I holds services there twic't a week and they bring me more food than I can eat. For instance, we's having chicken 'n' dumplin's tonight right after I pass around the hat."

"Preacher, you don't seem to be the average minister. I have always expected a pastor to visit the sick, the widows, the prisoners; perform weddings and more importantly do holy baptisms. Do you follow those traditions?" I asked.

"Oh yes, Mr. Cartah, I visits the sick all the time. I is very good to visit the widows and the prisoners. I knows most of them—they is my friends. In fact, many is kin folks. Now I performs weddings all the time. I gets a lot of business because I runs a special on that! I marries up them people but I offers them a 50% rebate if they gets a divorce!"

"How about baptisms?"

"I is known as the great dunker of all times. As a matter of fact, baptism is my best racket—er, I mean my best business—er, uh, service. That ceremony is sacred to my heart!"

"Well, Preacher, when did you last baptize someone?"

"Glad you asked. Last Sunday, up in Virginia, I held a big baptism. There was about 35 head to baptize. The deal is, the congregation on the shore takes up a collection to pay me. I charges 50 cents a head.

"I starts the baptisms whilst the congregation starts passin' around the bucket. If they don't come across with any money, I stops the baptism and tells 'em I ain't wettin' another damn nigger until I gets my money! "

The man had to be the world's greatest con artist! He was not dismayed at any warning about the extreme danger he might face; nor did he appear to be at all concerned that he might fail to make incriminating contact with the big shots in the whiskey business. He knew his rewards would depend on his success, however.

Agent Walden was to manage this undercover investigation. He was perfect for the job, being aggressive, highly trained and intelligent. If anyone could second-guess the preacher, Wally surely could.

Wally started the investigation by providing the reverend with enough government funds to make several purchases from medium sized violators.

He easily made purchases from the first violator he was assigned to. One outstanding case was his direct payment of marked money to Douglas Freeman Ross, one of the largest operators in the southeast. No such effort had ever been successful before.

We monitored the preacher's movements as closely as possible and knew he was not lying when he reported his purchases. He turned over the illegal whiskey to Wally and kept honest accounts of the government funds. In the back of my mind was a serious concern, however. Any informer or witness, when not backed up by a sworn officer's testimony in the ultimate criminal trial, is apt to lose the case because the defense counsel will attack his credibility. He will rake him over the coals and often will be able to provide evidence that the informant has a criminal record.

The defense invariably cross examines the federal agent managing an undercover investigation with reference to how much money an informant was paid. In this way he instills in the jurors' minds that the witness has lied in order to get subsistence and rewards. It has happened.

I have found that those seated on a jury panel with the serious responsibility of determining the guilt or innocence of a defendant are usually good and fair people. They are often reluctant to cause a person to go to prison on the testimony of only one witness who himself is much less than a saint.

Nevertheless, the preacher was making remarkable progress.

We decided it was time for him to attempt an undercover purchase from the smartest moonshiner of all, Percy Flowers.

I met with the preacher for over two hours. I explained our history of dispatching any and all available undercover operators in an attempt to catch Flowers. This included hired informants and new, unknown rookie agents—all to no avail.

It was not difficult for those teams to make direct purchases from Flowers' employees, who were considered his first lieutenants. Some of these subordinates were long trusted men who depended on Flowers for food, shelter and other elements of livelihood for their large families. His two most trusted aides were middle-aged black men, David Howard Creech and Sylvester Dixon.

I predicted that the preacher would never succeed in meeting or even seeing Flowers! Rev. Warlock was not convinced.

"Mr. Cartah, I will make such friends with his men that they will beg me to meet him!" he said.

"Well, Preacher, if you can get close to Flowers, you'll be the first," I told him.

"I can promise you that I will."

"I'll say one thing, Preacher. You surely are confident. After watching you for weeks I can understand why. You must have over a million friends!"

"Oh yeah, Mr. Cartah. I has more than a million friends and I loves 'em all! And I would like to sell every goddamn one of 'em for a dollah each!" he bragged.

As great as he thought he was, the preacher never got near Percy Flowers. He had no trouble purchasing illegal whiskey from several of Percy's hirelings, including Creech and Dixon; but even those hits were seriously flawed since the preacher was our only witness.

By this time the federal government had spent a lot of money on the operation. The preacher had about run his course with no hope of scoring against our principal target. The lack of corroborating evidence in any of the cases made it necessary to prosecute them in state court rather than U.S. district court.

After a detailed conference with an assistant district attorney for Johnston County, he selected one of the cases for prosecution as a test case. The idea was that if we were successful, other cases would be prosecuted.

The district attorney called the case against Jerry Coble, the preacher's first buy. Coble was represented by two of Johnston County's best attorneys.

Coble was a mere hireling of major violator Doug Ross. It was obvious that Ross would be paying the lawyers. It was also likely that Ross realized he could be arrested and taken to court since the preacher had also purchased 150 gallons of booze directly from him!

The preacher arrived a few minutes late. As usual, he was dressed like a New York stockbroker. All eyes were upon him as he strutted into the ancient court-room. Confident? No! More than that, he was cocky!

In this rural southern county the tentacles of the civil rights movement had made few inroads. In other words, to many of the spectators and maybe even some of the court officials, Rev. Warlock did not seem a very credible witness.

The prosecutor called the preacher to the stand. He was sworn to tell the truth, the whole truth and nothing but the truth.

Prosecutor: "Please state your name to the court."

Preacher: "I is Samuel P. Warlock, a Christian min-istah of the gospel. "

Prosecutor: "What is your present address?"

Preacher: "Well, suh, I lives on Route Three, Frank-lin County, in this great state of Virginia—I mean North Carolina."

Prosecutor: "What is your occupation?"

Preacher: "I is so pleased and humble to answer that question. You see, since my youth, I has been one of God's disciples. In my home state of Virginia, I covers the flock at the First Baptist Church at Bethel, near Richmond. The U.S. government has encouraged me to be an important instrument in suppression of the evil of illegal alcohol, which is the absolute ruina-tion of our total society. After prayerful meditation I realized I had to answer this call.

"So for several months I has risked my life, mixing with the dregs of humanity. That is to say, I buys illegal liquor from the most violent violators in the United

States. Mr. Walden and sometimes Mr. Cartah gives me the money to buy the liquor. I turns it over to them and then you see they brings these criminals into your honorable court and you sends their asses to prison."

Defense Attorney: "Your honor, we object to this witness making such comments. It seems he has already given very prejudiced testimony!"

Judge: "Objection sustained. Mr. Warlock, during the balance of this trial I do not want to hear any more of your speech making. Please answer only the questions asked."

Preacher: "I understands, Your Honah."

At that point the district attorney began the questioning concerning the buy from Coble. Rev. Warlock answered each question clearly and accurately.

Prosecutor: "My final question to you Reverend, is have you ever been convicted of a crime in any jurisdiction?"

Preacher: "Well, I surely must tell the whole truth, because the truth is the light and the light will set you free! When I was a small child I tried to relieve J.C. Penney Company in Richmond, Virginia of a overcoat. It was for my seventy-five year old grandmother. You see, it gets cold up there in Virginia in the wintertime. Granny was about to freeze 'cause she didn't have no coat, the poor soul! But I was only about 17 years old at the time."

Prosecutor: "Is there any other arrest or indictment in your background?"

Preacher: "Well, they most probably was a few times I was nailed for, but they didn't really amount to anything 'cause you see I won't guilty of any of them!"

By the time the assistant district attorney had completed his direct examination of our only witness, it was apparent we had screwed up royally in using this man. The district attorney glared at us as he returned to his seat. But this was not even the half of it. Now it was the defense counsel's turn!

Defense Attorney: "So you are a minister of the gospel?"

Preacher: "Oh yes. I was called to preach many years ago. Since that time, I has covered the flock at many places."

Defense Attorney: "Well, tell us, when you get 'called' to preach, is that a voice from the air and that's all?"

Preacher: "Well now, that's mostly it, but being a man of complete truth I will say that the hot sun beatin' down on my back in those Virginia cotton fields did have a little something to do with it."

Defense Attorney: "I will not take up the valuable time of the court by asking the many questions I would ordinarily ask of such a person as you. On the other hand, for the record I will ask you about what I'm holding in my hand—that is, an FBI record showing something like 17 charges that have been brought against you over the past few years!

"These charges range from trespassing and non-support of minor children to extortion, burglary, forgery, embezzlement, larceny and fraud. What do you have to say about that?"

Preacher: "Well, that do look bad but given the opportunity to do so I can explain those things. For example, the terrible charge of nonsupport, as bad as it appears, was brought against me by one of the sistahs in the flock I covers at Bethel. She done went out and got knocked up by some other man and didn't remember who he was, so she blamed it on me."

Defense Attorney: "What about these other charges?"

Preacher: "Well, suh, I believes you mentioned larceny, meaning that I stole something. I admit that when I was very young, maybe not over 18 years old, I was walking down the road one day on my way to help take up some money for the Red Cross. I saw a rope layin' on the shoulder of the road. Well, suh, thinking that somebody done throwed that rope away, I just picked it up. I didn't realize there was a cow on the other end of the rope. So they 'cused me of stealing the cow!

"Now if you will, suh, repeat them other offenses that I's 'cused up with. I can explain them, too—"

Defense Attorney: "Never mind the others! I don't even want to hear any more and I'm sure the judge doesn't either.

"Your Honor, this witness is not sufficiently credible to send my client to jail or to prison for any crime."

Preacher: "But suh, I must implore the court to hear my answer to those false charges that has been read to you!"

Judge: "Mr. Warlock, I'm not impressed with you but I will give you the benefit of the doubt. I'll give you a couple more minutes to answer the argument about your past record."

Preacher: "The charge of burglary, Your Honah. Now, I did become a guest of the state for almost three years when they thought I broke into that shop—I believe it was a pawn shop—up in Richmond. Your Honah, the truth of that is, and the truth is the light, and the light will set you free, that I was up that street attending a prayer session. As I was walking back to my car, I stumbled in front of that shop and accidentally fell against the plate glass window, breaking it.

"Being a man of God—you know, honest to the core—I just couldn't walk off and leave that place wide open for them thieving mother-fuckers that was all over the place. So you see I crawled through that broken glass and went to the cash register where I thought I would find something to write with. While I was looking a policeman came in and busted me! I was only trying to leave my name and address so they would know I wanted to pay for the broken glass!"

Judge: "Mr. Prosecuting Attorney, just where in the holy hell did you come up with such a witness for the state or the U.S. government? Did you hear the language used by this man—a man who claims to be a minister of the gospel? I am tempted at this point to throw out the case. First, however, I will hear from you! The jury is excused for 30 minutes!"

During the recess, the embarrassed prosecutor addressed the judge. "Your Honor, I am caught at this point without appropriate words. I can only move that the court dismiss the case against the defendant and humbly apologize to Your Honor for this fiasco. I promise that never again will my office fall victim to such an action.

"I will consult with the federal agents who initiated this case. In their defense, Your Honor, I'm sure they are as troubled over this as we are. I know their reputations well. This is totally out of character for them. I can only assume that this so-called 'minister of the gospel' conned them as he did the rest of us."

"Case dismissed," said the judge.

# TWO GUN PETE

A friend of mine, a Chicago Homicide detective, told this story several years ago. I think it is an ideal story relating to *Shortcuts to Justice*.

He told of a huge black policeman in the police department with the nickname "Two Gun Pete." He was known by that name because of his habit of carrying a second handgun concealed in his shoe or under his clothing. He did so in order to shoot a suspect if he so desired and claim self-defense by planting the hidden gun on the body of the victim, in the event that said victim had no weapon of his own. In telling this story, my friend said, "Christ, he killed niggers that didn't even need killing!" (As if that would be difficult to do.)

On a particular occasion, my friend and his partner responded to a report of a shooting in the "Black Belt" area of Chicago. On arrival at the location given, they found a dead man with a bullet hole between his eyes. The only other person present was an elderly woman. When asked if she knew who had killed the man, she said, "Well suh, I think it was that black officer, Mr. Two Gun Pete."

Pete was not on the scene, but drove up in his patrol car about thirty minutes later. He took a cheap handgun from his pocket, threw it on the corpse and declared, "Well, see, I had to shoot the muther cause he pointed that gun at me."

"My God," said my friend, "the son-of-a-bitch had forgotten the gun that day and had to go back home to get it!"

This technique is known as the "dropper" and is somewhat illegal, especially in these modern times.

# LEGAL EAGLE—HOBE MORTON, ESQ.

W e will not call peckers 'cucumbers', nor pussies 'cauliflowers' during this trial, ladies and gentlemen. My client is wrongly accused of rape and is on trial for his life. We are desperate and will defend him with great vigor. We will not substitute polite words for impolite ones. If you can't hack this I suggest you leave now!"

The person who delivered this blunt and shocking message in the Superior Courtroom of Stanly County in Albemarle, North Carolina was Hobart Morton, Esq., a middle-aged attorney and already a legendary practitioner of defensive criminal law. A native of that area, he was widely known as an oratorical genius who could get you off if you had plenty of money, no matter what the crime involved.

When I was about eight years old my father took me to some sort of political function of the local Republican party at which attorney Morton was a guest speaker. I remember that long-ago occasion because of his ability to spellbind his listeners, his subject notwithstanding.

"We must icicle the damn Democrats out of office. They have been sucking the teats of the American taxpayers long enough!" I heard more new words that day than I later heard all during high school.

During his summary the audience was invited to ask questions or offer comments. One young man asked, "Mr. Morton, you speak good of Republicans but very bad about Democrats. Don't you believe that I should vote for the man and not just for the party?"

"Son, I always vote for the man, but I always make DAMN sure the man is a Republican before I vote for him!"

When Morton later defended Marvin Calcote, the client charged with the capital crime of rape of one Ann Roper, the penalty under the laws of North Carolina was death for that crime. It is no longer considered a capital crime in this state and as far as I know, in any other state. In fact, a convicted rapist is not likely to serve much time in prison, sometimes being released within months. In my opinion, the death penalty should not only be reinstated for that crime, but should also be USED!

Marvin Calcote was 40 years old at the time of the alleged rape. He owned a small farm several miles from town and lived alone, his wife having disappeared years before.

It was common knowledge in the community that Calcote was a moonshiner and that he produced the best pure corn whiskey in the territory. It was widely believed that he sold a large portion of his illegal product to the most prominent people, lawyer Morton being one of his best customers.

Calcote was an expert in the camouflage and concealment of illicit distilleries. Nevertheless, the local sheriff and federal ATF agents would occasionally find one and destroy it. For some strange reason they could not catch Calcote at the scene.

That is, not until the time the sheriff was out of the county for a week attending the Sheriff's Association convention in the capital. He didn't know federal agents would be conducting a raid during his absence. They found the still in operation and by the light of a full Carolina moon arrested two men, one being the elusive Calcote.

That was his first conviction in federal court, which ordinarily resulted in a probationary sentence for a first offense in a liquor case. The agents testified that Calcote was a major and frequent violator of the federal liquor laws. The judge sentenced him to one year and one day.

Calcote had a record of several other state arrests for assault, drunk and disorderly and assault on a woman. The latter charge was brought against him by his wife, who refused to press charges in many like incidents. At this trial she testified that he had beaten her often; that on most of those occasions he had been drinking heavily; and furthermore that he treated her savagely (especially sexually), his behavior to her being equivalent to continuous rape.

It was for this crime that Calcote received his second prison sentence, to be served at a state prison, better known as the chain gang.

As he was being escorted from the courtroom he cursed his wife and promised her he would even the score.

Calcote was released several weeks before completing his sentence. Although his wife had been seen regularly in the community during his absence, no one remembered ever seeing her after his release. The mystery of her sudden disappearance spawned many suspicions and rumors and was never resolved. The answer given by Calcote to those brave souls who dared ask about her was always, "Don't know where she is. The bitch had cleared out when I got back." Most people believe he killed his wife; however, there was no investigation and consequently no evidence.

Ann Roper, the alleged victim in the rape case, was 39 years old. She was rather tall with blond hair and considered quite attractive. She had moved to Stanly County only two or three years before and stayed away from public activities. No one in the community knew much about her except that she associated frequently with Marvin Calcote.

It was therefore less than shocking to see her enter the local magistrate's office one afternoon in a disheveled and bruised condition.

Within 20 minutes Sheriff Efird, two deputies and the local district attorney arrived at the magistrate's office. Shortly thereafter an ambulance appeared. Ann Roper and one of the deputies departed in the ambulance. The sheriff, the other deputy and the district attorney followed closely behind.

Early the next morning the citizens of Stanly County were entertained with the news that Marvin

Calcote was in the local jail charged with the capital offense of rape of his alleged girlfriend, Ann Roper.

By noon it was widely known that Hobe Morton had been retained to defend Calcote. On the second day of his incarceration, Calcote was to appear at a preliminary hearing in District Court. To the astonishment of everyone, Mr. Morton waived the right to a preliminary hearing and Calcote was bound over to the next term of Superior Court for trial.

The standing-room-only crowd of spectators expressed a loud, "Aw, Shit!" There were two probable reasons for this: the always-prevalent morbid curiosity and passion concerning the dilemma of other humans and disappointment at missing a portion of attorney Morton's entertaining courtroom performance.

It is probable that Morton was merely exercising one of his many smart strategies in waiving preliminary hearing, making it unnecessary for the victim to display her recently inflicted bruises to the large crowd packed into the courtroom.

After all it was certain that some of those citizens would ultimately serve on the jury at Calcote's trial. Morton did not wish any prospective jurors to remember Ann Roper's battered face.

Calcote was denied bond and remained in jail until the trial. Attorney Morton visited him often, trying to secure Calcote's cooperation in planning the defense.

The trial was scheduled to begin at 10:00 a.m. on the first Monday in October, 1935. The courtroom was completely filled hours before that, over half the spectators being women. For that reason Morton requested permission from presiding judge Phillips to address the audience. Permission was granted and Morton made the shocking statement mentioned above. A wave of laughter was the only result. Not one person left the courtroom.

The process of jury selection began with subpoenas to appear in court on the appointed date. On instruction by the judge the Clerk of Superior Court Norman Chaffee read the *venire*, a list of citizens who according to public records were not convicted felons and who paid their county property taxes on time.

A majority of those summoned did not like the idea of serving on a jury at all and especially not in a case like this in which a man was on trial for his life. All kinds of requests to be excused from that responsibility were heard and for that matter always will be.

On the other hand, there will always be a few people who are eager to serve.

Monday, Tuesday, Wednesday and Thursday of the first week were completely consumed in selecting a jury. The normal monotony of jury selection was broken by Morton's courtroom conduct, which was unorthodox at best and outrageous at its worst. In either mode he was effective and covered the legal waterfront one way or the other.

The selection of a jury in any trial is very crucial. The Morton star shone at its brightest during this procedure. He appeared to have rare instincts bordering on reading the minds of potential jurors.

His scrutiny and questioning of each juror was skillful to the point of intimidation.

If convicted for the crime of rape, Morton's client could be given the death penalty. Although confident that he could beat the prosecution, Morton left no stone unturned and no questions unasked of any prospective juror before accepting him.

Attorney Morton: "J.P., I've known you for a long time. Everyone knows that you are an ideal citizen with good common sense but it is obvious as a result of questions asked of you by the prosecutor that you had rather not serve on this jury. When Mr. Sharp asked you for your reasons for not wanting to serve you simply said that you did not have enough education to be a juror. It does not require any certain amount of education so much as good, fair judgment and common sense. I will ask you how far you did go in school?"

J.P.: "Well, I can't rightly say, except I went as far as you can get in three months."

Morton: "J.P., that's not such a good answer. I once asked a juror how much education he had. He said, 'Not much, but I always say those who have no education have to use our heads!' Now if you serve here in this trial, we just want you to 'use your head!'

"Now, J.P., a while ago you indicated that there was another reason why you should be excused. Please tell the court about that."

J.P.: "It's very embarrassing, Mr. Morton. Let me just slide on that and say that I'm not well!"

Morton: "Now, J.P., the court will need to know. We're all human and mature humans at that, so out with it."

J.P.: "Wal, if ya have to know, I've been constipated for two weeks."

Morton: "You should have seen a doctor. He could have given you something to solve your problem."

J.P.: "I did go see him last week. He gave me something called suppositories. I took the last one this morning. Didn't help at all. For all the good they done, I may as well have been stickin' 'em up my ass!"

A burst of laughter filled the courtroom. When the judge finally stopped laughing he said, "J.P., you are excused from jury duty and I suggest that you go back to your doctor and ask him just how you take such medication."

Only three jurors were selected on the first day out of eleven who were called and interviewed. Both sides were vying intently for jurors who would lean their way.

On the second day no one was chosen until the afternoon. The first potential juror called for questioning in the afternoon was an elderly widow by the name of Ester May Kirk.

District Attorney Sharp: "Mrs. Kirk, as you may recall, his honor has announced that the defendant is on trial for the crime of rape, a capital offense. Now I must ask you—and please contemplate your answer before you give it—do you believe in capital punishment?"

Mrs. Kirk: "Oh, yes I most certainly do, if it's not too severe!"

Prosecutor: "You may step down Mrs. Kirk, the state does not need you."

After Mrs. Kirk was dismissed four more jurors were seated. At the end of the second day seven had been accepted, leaving five to go.

On the third day three others were accepted, leaving only two to go.

Thursday saw another elderly lady called. She was Annabelle Lefler, the wife of a prominent farmer.

Attorney Morton: "Mrs. Lefler, have you formed any opinion in this case as to the guilt or innocence of Mr. Calcote?"

Mrs. Lefler: "Well, I don't personally know him but I do know our good Christian sheriff. I'm positive that Mr. Calcote is guilty because I know our sheriff would not have arrested him and brought him in here if he had been innocent!"

Morton: "Your Honor, the defendant must reject this lady."

Next to be called was Luther Stokes, a farmer about forty years old who lived with his wife in a nearby community.

After a few routine questions, all apparently being satisfactorily answered, the prosecutor asked his final question.

Prosecutor: "Now Mr. Stokes, do you know of any reason why you may not be able to render a fair decision for either the state or the defendant in this case?"

Mr. Stokes: "I do not know of any, right off hand."

Prosecutor: "Are you familiar with the term 'circumstantial evidence,' and if so, do you believe in it?"

Mr. Stokes: "Oh Lord no, I sure don't."

Prosecutor: "Will you please tell the court why you do not."

Mr. Stokes: "Well, I don't like to talk about it but I suppose I'll have to, since this is a trial.

"You see, my wife and I live on our farm out near Lizzard Lick. We raise hogs and cattle as well as corn, cotton and wheat. Well, one day I went into the barn to feed a half-grown heifer some ground grain. I opened the door to the stall and was standing in the doorway when all of a sudden I felt the need to piss. About the time I got my ding-a-ling out, the stupid animal charged by me to escape to the wide open spaces. As she passed me I just automatically grabbed her by the tail.

"There I was running across the barnyard with one hand still on my pecker and holding the heifer by the tail with the other hand, running like the devil to keep up with the bitch.

"The worst part was that my wife was looking out the kitchen window and saw the whole damn thing. Do you think I was ever able to convince her that I was innocent? And you ask me if I believe in circumstantial evidence?"

Prosecutor: "You are excused, Mr. Stokes."

Next to be called was a young hardware store clerk named Herman Trull. He was an activist strongly opposed to the legal or illegal sale of any kind of alcoholic beverage.

Attorney Morton knew of Trull's bias concerning this and was wary of him for that reason. He knew the prosecution would try to bring out Calcote's involvement with whiskey, both his consumption and making of it.

Morton was concerned that many people were so hypocritical on the subject that it was difficult to discern how one would react when placed in a situation where he might hold the power of life or death.

Attorney Morton was a drinking man and made no secret of it. He had lived among these people all his life and was well aware of the opinions voiced in public by a majority of them. The locality was well within the Southern Bible Belt where the use of alcohol in any form was looked upon as a no-no. The Protestant churches had forever taught that alcohol was evil, a substance of the devil and to be avoided.

In reality however, many of those devout church people who publicly fought against the use of alcohol were definitely not against it in the privacy of their homes. Some kept a jug in a convenient place such as behind the hat box on the top shelf of a bedroom closet.

I believe it was Will Rogers who said, "The Baptists will vote dry as long as they can stagger to the polls." However as time goes by, things change. The Baptists are much more liberal now. They will speak to each other when they accidentally meet in the liquor store.

Although Morton was apprehensive about Herman Trull, he was concerned that the few remaining persons who had been subpoenaed did not look very promising. He had a small trick up his sleeve. Herman Trull was questioned at length by the prosecutor, who was satisfied with him.

Attorney Morton: "Herman, are you a happily married man?"

Herman Trull: "Oh yessir, Mr. Morton, we are both very happy."

Morton: "Herman, what do you think of a man who will sleep with a woman and then eat her cooking?"

Trull: "Well, I'd think he'd be a very bad man or one who was drunk and oughta be locked up!"

Morton: "Now think about it for a moment Herman. You probably sleep with your wonderful wife, don't you?"

Trull: "Well, sure, but..."

Morton: "And you eat what she cooks for you, don't you?"

Trull: "O-O-Oh yeah. I do, I was not thinkin' that question through. It was not what it seemed to be."

Morton: "Thank you, Herman. That's the point I want to make. I was not by any means trying to embarrass you. You gave a good answer when you said the question was not what it first seemed to be. I think you will be a good and fair juror. My point in asking you that tricky question was to help you to wisely evaluate all testimony in this trial. You can see now, as you said, 'that question was not what it seemed to be.' Perhaps some of those you will hear during this trial won't be, either."

Herman Trull was accepted, completing the jury of eight men and four women. Attorney Morton was very pleased with all of them but most of the others involved in the trial were very displeased with Mr.

Morton. Of course, the spectators enjoyed every m-inute of his antics and there was still standing room only.

At this point the judge adjourned court until the next day. He instructed attorney Morton to join him in his chambers for a few moments. No one knew for sure what their secret meeting was about but most people assumed the judge warned Morton about his court-room tactics.

When the court reconvened the following day the jury was sworn and seated.

After the legal preliminaries, the superior court judge invited opening statements by the prosecution and defense. The solicitor delivered the usual impor-tant but monotonous brief on the crime. He explained how the state would present evidence more than ade-quate to convict the defendant of the awful crime of rape.

When the prosecutor had completed his opening address, the crowd of spectators became noticeably more alert. There was no doubt that this was due to the reputation of the counsel for the defense.

Attorney Hobart Morton strode to the podium facing the spectators. The courtroom lights shone on his silvery hair. His magnetic smile in place, he turned his head toward the judge and requested that he be allowed to deliver his opening statement.

Judge: "Mr. Morton, approach the bench."

Attorney Morton (approaching the bench): "What is it, Your Honor?"

Judge: "Mr. Morton, I have long been aware of your effective but sometimes risky courtroom tactics. Your antics during the selection of this jury worry me to some extent. I am somewhat uncomfortable with the way you handled certain people on the jury. Therefore, before we proceed I will ask your client if he is satisfied with this jury. I do not do this out of disrespect or lack of trust in your judgment. I must be very careful to see that justice is fully served and that all possibilities are eliminated concerning a mistrial. In the event of a conviction of your client I do not want to cause grounds for you to appeal. Do you understand?"

Attorney Morton: "Your Honor, I have a problem with what you said. Yes, I do understand and that's the problem I have with what you said. However, you're the boss (at least until the next election)."

Morton returned to the defense table. He told Calcote that the judge was going to ask him a question. "For God's sake, Marvin, stand up when he speaks to you and don't say anything to make the old bastard angry."

Judge: "Mr. Calcote, the question I am about to ask you is not about any evidence nor any other aspect of this trial. On the other hand it has to do with my responsibility as a judge. This is particularly important in assuring that you and the defendants in all cases get a fair trial. Do you understand, Mr. Calcote?"

Marvin Calcote: "Uh-huh—I mean yeah."

Judge: "Here is my question. Mr. Morton is satisfied with the jury. Are you sure that you are satisfied with the jury?"

Calcote: "Judge, that's a dumb-ass question! How the hell do you expect me to be satisfied wit dem jurors until I see whedder they turn't me loose or hung me?"

Judge: "Mr. Calcote, I will not tolerate any more foul language or disrespect in my court!

"Now, let me put it another way. I want you to look over all the jurors seated here and say whether or not you would like to challenge any of them."

Calcote was energized by this offer. He smiled and paced importantly back and forth in front of the jury, enjoying the instant power. Again and again, he eye-balled each of the twelve jurors. Finally he responded.

Calcote: "Judge, I will challenge that little old man on the far end of the back row. I think I can lick him."

The judge finally managed to restore order by letting the loud laughter subside.

Judge: "Mr. Calcote, that is not the kind of challenge I was talking about. Go back to your seat and let Mr. Morton straighten you out. Apparently he knows his job better than I know mine."

After a lengthy recess, Morton addressed the court.

Attorney Morton: "Your Honor, ladies and gentlemen of the jury and all others who have an interest in this case, based on a God-given hunger for the fair and proper administration of justice for all. Listen up!

"As you have seen, my client is not quite like you and me. You may have noticed in his response to our wise and illustrious judge, uh, well–uh–you know what I mean, he tries to row his boat with one oar.

"That is something he was born with, (or maybe I should say, that he was born without). In any case it is sad that this poor underprivileged man, whom Mother Nature has so tragically short changed, although completely honest, a model citizen and 100% innocent of the horrible crime he is so unjustly charged with, is even here in the first place.

"The state will bust a gut to prove that my client Mr. Calcote committed the awful crime of rape of Ann Roper. We will show that he is innocent and that she is a pathological liar, unworthy of belief.

"Now with his honor's permission, I wish to describe the morbid destination the state has in mind for this simple and innocent man. Do you know that the penalty for the crime of rape in this state can be death? Do you know how the state of North Carolina dispatches its condemned people? Undoubtedly you have heard of our electric chair but have you heard how it works? Probably not! Well, let me enlighten you!"

Judge: "Mr. Morton, watch it! You are about to risk stepping across the line."

Attorney Morton: "Thank you Your Honor. I merely want these fine jurors to realize they may hold this man's life or a horrible death in their hands. I wish them to realize how very serious this responsibility is—all of course, in the interest of justice, Your Honor!"

Judge: "Proceed, but please don't get out of line."

Morton: "Thank you Your Honor. Now ladies and gentlemen of the jury, only a few more minutes and we can get on with the rumors and outright lies that the prosecutor will call 'evidence.'"

District Attorney: "Your Honor, I object. As usual, Mr. Morton is attempting to brainwash the members of the jury, intimidate them and even make them feel guilty with an exaggerated and morbid description of the state's method of execution."

Judge: "Objection overruled. I am, however, just about to ask him to end his opening statement. For now, Mr. Morton, continue."

Attorney Morton: "Ladies and gentlemen of the jury, as you can see the prosecutor is trying to conceal from you what you will cause my client to suffer if you find him guilty.

"Let me begin by not mentioning the day by day torture of death row and go on to the prison routine of the condemned. He eats his last meal on the eve of his execution. Twenty-four hours prior, his head is shaved as slick as a peeled onion. This enables the stainless steel cap or helmet to effectively conduct several thousand electrical volts throughout his body. Before he begins his last mile a watertight rubber diaper is placed on him so his feces and urine will not mess up the area. His ankles and wrists are then strapped to the chair. A black hood is placed over his head. Then as a morbid crowd of witnesses looks on, the warden nods his head and the executioner pulls the switch. Blisters instantly pop out on the condemned one's forehead, face and neck. The rubber diaper is suddenly filled; the strong leather straps holding him in the chair are stretched nearly to the breaking point. A sickening odor of barbecued flesh, scorched hair and body waste fills the room. The current stops and what is left of a human being becomes limp. The switch is pulled again and the corpse jumps erect again, as if it were still alive.

"Ladies and gentlemen of the jury, this is not the first time I have fought to save a man's life. I have lost on only a couple of occasions and won many times.

"You probably can't imagine how it makes an attorney feel to lose in a capital case. It is always very sad. I can remember almost verbatim the condemned man's last words. I especially recall one young colored man whose upbeat spirit and sense of humor never failed him.

"On the eve of his execution, the warden visited him to ask what he would like for his last meal. Although it was mid-January and cold as a polar bear's hemorrhoids, the young man said, 'Well, Boss, I believe I'll have watermelon!'

"'Hell, man, you know it's winter and there will be no watermelons for several months!'

"'Well,' replied my client, 'that's okay, Boss, I can wait.'

"Ladies and gentlemen, his honor will instruct each of you to listen closely to all of the evidence. Then when the state and the defense have completed their evidence, his honor will charge you. This does not mean that he will charge you a fee, it means that he will go to great lengths to guide you by explaining the law, in effect telling you what you can consider. He will completely summarize all the points of evidence offered by both sides.

Officers check out the engine on a hot rod liquor car. Note Dual carburetors on the flathead Ford engine.

Joe Carter talks with other officers in still yard after raid.

Legendary ATF agent Sam Cabe at large moonshine still in Wilkes County, North Carolina.

"Snuffy Smith" type distillery seized in Wilkes County, N.C. in 1958. Author is second from right in photo.

"Ending my opening statement, let me say that I will provide sufficient evidence to enable you to find my client not guilty."

The judge declared the trial adjourned until the following Monday at 9:00 a.m.

Attorney Morton had his work cut out for him. He had only two days to fully prepare his case for the defendant. By now he realized Marvin Calcote would be of very little assistance. After all, Calcote's response to Judge Phillips concerning his right to challenge the jury indicated that he was a mental midget. Morton would have to play it by ear.

On Saturday morning, Morton visited Calcote in his jail cell for the purpose of planning (or plotting) the defense.

"Marvin, now listen up. We have a very serious situation and it's a matter of life or death for you. All day today and maybe tomorrow, we must work up a strategy here.

"For some reason, I get the idea you aren't taking this trial too seriously! Now I'm telling you, by God, you'd better get serious! If you don't I'm going to ask the judge to relieve me as your lawyer! If that happens the court will appoint some half-ass young lawyer to represent you. The state will pay him a low fee and he will get your ass hung.

"I would be pissed at you even if you were paying me, which you ain't. I'll be frank with you, Marvin. Part of my motivation in defending you is that you do make the best corn liquor in this part of the state.

"Now let's start off with you telling me just how this case came about and whether you are guilty—which you probably are. If you are guilty, we've got to figure out how to make you innocent."

Calcote replied, "Well, I ain't guilty of no rape. I have been shackin' up with her ever now and then for years. But I shore as hell ain't never took it away from her. She does a lot of fuckin' with a lot of men, but she does it for money. Every time I been with her I always paid for it. That is except for this time, which she has LAWED me for. I done some work on her old car that I figured she owed me for. She said she didn't have the money and won't goin' to pay me so I decided to screw it out of her. She won't too happy with that but she finally went along with it."

"How do you explain the fact that she was beaten up, man?" asked Morton. "You know the prosecutor will show the jury color photos of her face and body. He'll try to make it look like you ran over her with a log truck."

"Well, I shore didn't make her look like that," said Calcote. "A man who came to see me after I was 'rested by them crooked deputies told me that the night after I was with her she put on a gang bangin' with 13 men under ole Curtis Creek Bridge. Maybe some of them fellers beat her up."

After a full day of preparing for the trial, Morton was confident he could beat the rap. He planned to spend the rest of the weekend searching for witnesses who may have been involved in the gang banging suggested by Calcote. He also briefed Calcote on the possibility of putting him on the witness stand, but only as a last resort.

Morton had heard enough about Ann Roper from Calcote and others that he felt confident he could destroy her credibility during cross-examination, once the prosecution had presented her to the court as its principal witness.

By 7:00 a.m. on Monday, two hours before the judge was to reconvene the court for the trial of Marvin Calcote, a line of people more than sufficient to fill the courtroom formed on the street near the courthouse. Most of the sheriff's deputies were on hand to assure order.

At 8:30 a.m. the court bailiff opened the doors and the public rushed in, frantically grabbing for seats.

At exactly 9:00 a.m. Superior Court Judge Phillips, a very distinguished and stately man, entered the courtroom from his adjacent chambers.

Bailiff: "All rise! Oyez! Oyez! This court is now in session, the Honorable Sam Phillips presiding. Be seated."

Thereafter, with the spectators reseated, the trial began.

Judge: "Mr. District Attorney, you may call your first witness."

Prosecutor: "Thank you, Your Honor. The state calls Ann Roper to the witness stand. Be sworn, Mrs. Roper."

Mrs. Roper was sworn and the questioning began.

Prosecutor: "State your full name, please."

Witness: "Ann Maner Copeland Roper."

Prosecutor: "Are you now married?"

Witness: "No sir, I have been married twic't and divorced twic't."

Prosecutor: "Where do you now reside?"

Witness: "I live alone in a mobile home on Route 3, Palmertown."

Prosecutor: "Are you employed, and if so, where?"

Witness: "I do house cleaning for different people. Ya know, kinda free lance stuff."

Prosecutor: "Do you know the defendant, Marvin Calcote?"

Witness: "Yeah, sorta."

Prosecutor: "What do you mean, 'sorta'?"

Witness: "Well, I met 'im at a square dance a while back."

Prosecutor: "Go ahead and tell his honor and the jury how you happened to meet him. Describe what you know about him including any relationship you have had with him."

Witness: "Well, like I said, I went to a pig pickin' and square dance at George Nash's house, uh-long about last September, I reckin. Marvin was thar and got to talkin' to me. I reckin he musta sorta liked my looks. Ya see, I was wearin' my tight britches and a pullover sweater. Well, he just kept follerin' me around and tellin' me how good I looked. Once't or twic't he patted me on the butt. But I dint get mad, 'cause he was drinkin' right smart. They told me he made the liquor for the party—"

Attorney Morton (interrupting the witness): "I object, Your Honor. That's hearsay. Move to strike."

Judge: "Objection sustained. Ladies and gentlemen of the jury, I instruct you to disregard the testimony of this witness as to her hearsay statement."

Morton: "Thank you, Your Honor."

Prosecutor: "Proceed, Mrs. Roper. Tell the court everything you know that relates to this trial but not what you heard someone other than Mr. Calcote say."

Witness: "Well, like I said, he just follered me around that time. He ast me where I lived and what I did fer a livin'. I told him I do house cleanin' for people and where I lived. He ast me if I would hire out to do housework for him an' I told 'im I'd think about it."

Prosecutor: "Well, Mrs. Roper, did you ever hire out to Mr. Calcote?"

Witness: "Uh-huh I did and that's when he raped me. I mean, not the first time I cleaned his house. It was right much later when he did it."

Prosecutor: "Go ahead and tell the court in detail exactly what happened. Now please take your time."

Witness: "Well, it happened that Friday night. I went to his house to clean. He won't home at first so I went ahead and started. It won't long, 'bout first dark when he showed up. He wuz drinkin' heavy and actin' mean. I told him iffn' he dint shut his tater trap I was goin' to leave and I told him he still hadn't paid me fer the last time. Well sir, he sho 'nuff did break bad then! He cussed me good, uh–er–uh, he said, 'you damn slut, I fixed your damn ole car and you dint pay me fer it. So by God, I'm fixin' to take it out in trade right now.' Then he knocked me down and drug me into the bedroom and tore my clothes off, yanked off his britches and raped me!"

Prosecutor: "Now Mrs. Roper, tell the court what happened next."

Witness: "Well, after he raped me, he kept drinkin' his moonshine 'till he passed out. So I took my car and left for home. The next day I went to town and reported what happent."

The prosecutor continued his questioning of the witness for about another hour. During this time he established what he thought were all the facts necessary to withstand what he knew from experience would be a defensive blitz by attorney Morton.

Judge Phillips recessed the trial until 2:00 p.m.

To the crowd of spectators, 2:00 p.m. meant SHOW TIME! The legal giant Hobart Morton would begin his cross-examination of the state's principal witness. His performance would determine the fate of Marvin Calcote. To win meant freedom; to lose, death.

Fearful of losing their seats, some of the spectators declined to go out for lunch. Others rushed out, grabbed a very quick snack and hurried back to the courtroom.

Small wagers were made in great numbers by the spectators. Odds as high as five to one were offered that Calcote would be acquitted.

A majority expected that attorney Morton would actually conduct a verbal lynching of Ann Roper upon cross-examining her.

The trial resumed at 2:00 p.m.

Judge: "Mr. Prosecutor, did you have more questions to ask this witness, Mrs. Ann Roper?"

Prosecutor: "No, Your Honor. Your witness, Mr. Morton."

Ann Roper returned to the witness stand.

Attorney Morton: "Mrs. Roper, you realize that you are under oath to tell the truth, don't you?"

Witness: "Yeah—I do."

Morton: "And you do know that if you lie while under oath, you'll be committing a crime known as perjury, don't you?"

Witness: "Yeah."

Morton placed his hands on the witness box, leaned toward the witness until his face was only inches from hers and in a tone of voice that would make coffee nervous said, "Then you must know that a lie here while you are under oath could net you five years in jail."

Witness: "What makes you think I'm gonna lie? I don't like how ya bin talkin' to me!"

Prosecutor: "Your Honor I object! Mr. Morton is badgering the witness by trying to frighten her out of her wits!"

Judge: "Sustained. Mr. Morton, it is unnecessary to try to intimidate the witness by reminding her of the criminal penalty for a crime she has not committed. Get on with your questions and make sure they relate to the issues at hand!"

Morton: "Yes, Your Honor. Now, Mrs. Roper, I believe you testified that you met Mr. Calcote at a barn dance."

Witness: "Naw, I said it was a square dance."

Morton: "Well, no matter, barn dance or square dance, it's the same. Now are you sure that's the first time you had seen or met him? And that was last September?"

Witness: "Shore was and I wish I hadn't met the skunk at all!"

Morton: "Now you testified, did you not, that you then took a job with Mr. Calcote, housekeeping for him?"

Witness: "It won't like a full job. I would jist go clean his house onc't in a while, maybe like onc't a week."

Morton: "Now according to your grand jury testimony, on the last occasion you went to clean his house he assaulted you and raped you, on or about May 18 of this year."

Witness: "Yeah."

Morton: "But the prosecutor, our District Attorney Sharp, on his direct questioning did not ask you how many times you had been to Mr. Calcote's home prior to the time that you say he raped you. Now I'm asking you, how many times had you been to his house to clean, or whatever it was you really went there for?"

Prosecutor: "I object, Your Honor. The witness has already testified that she only went there to clean the house."

Morton: "Not so, Your Honor. The District Attorney has not asked her if she went there for any other reason!"

Judge: "Overruled. Mr. Morton, you may propose that question to her."

Morton: "Thank you, Your Honor. Mrs. Roper, now tell the court if you only went there to clean house—or isn't it a fact that this was an arrangement like many others whereby a woman cooks and does for a man without being married, but just like a married couple?"

Witness: "Well–uh–onc't in a while I cooked there, but that's all!"

Morton: "Mrs. Roper I ask you again, about how many times did you go to Mr. Calcote's house to do whatever you did, from the first time last September until this time that was on or about May 18 of this year?"

Witness: "I don't rightly know, I awready said it was about onc't a week."

Morton: "I ask you—and remember you are under oath—did you stay overnight at his house, with him there?"

Witness: (In a shrill voice) "I did a few times but I didn't sleep with 'im, if that's what you're drivin' at, you ole puzzle-gutted bastard!"

(Attorney Morton was delighted with his progress in this cross-examination. He had the witness thoroughly rattled and knew she would now be completely irrational in her responses.)

Judge: "The witness will refrain from such crude name-calling forthwith."

Morton: "I forgive the witness, Your Honor. I gave up trying to be as attractive as Mr. America long ago."

Judge: "You may continue, Mr. Morton."

Morton: "Mrs. Roper, you testified that on May 18 you went to the home of Marvin Calcote to clean the house and that he was not at home. You testified further that you went in and started to clean anyway. Now, I ask you if his house was locked?"

Witness: "Yeah, it was."

Morton: "I assume that you did not break in so you must have had a key, is that correct?"

Witness: "Yeah, I had a key! Is there anything wrong with that?"

Morton: "I didn't say there was anything wrong with it. As a matter of fact, I think it's real nice to be so intimate with a person and to show such wholesome trust as sharing a house—well, as sharing a key for a house."

The deadly questioning by the defense counsel worried the prosecutor. Hoping to have a private conference with his star witness to calm her and to enhance his position, he asked the judge for a recess until the following day. The judge obliged.

After the trial was recessed for the day the prosecutor had a serious conference with Ann Roper. He tried to reassure her and encourage her to remain calm under the third degree questioning by attorney Morton. He also informed her that Morton was probably the most dreaded lawyer in the country. He implored her to hold herself together and assured her that he would continue to object to Morton's every effort to frustrate her. The judge would protect her from abuse.

The trial resumed at 10:00 a.m. the following day. Ann Roper returned to the witness stand for further cross-examination.

Attorney Morton: "Good morning to you, Mrs. Roper. I do hope you had a very good night's sleep!"

Witness: "Yeah, I bet you do. I don't see how you can sleep at all."

Morton: "Oh, ho-ho Mrs. Roper, you shouldn't feel that way. I'm just an honest old country lawyer trying to see that innocent people like Mr. Calcote can enjoy justice and liberty, for which I barely earn a living."

Witness: "Bull! He ain't innocent and you ain't honest or poor! He'll pay you with that rot-gut whiskey he makes and you'll sell it to whoever's got the dough."

The attorney was pleased with her hostility, knowing he still had her in such an emotional state that additional and intensified cross-examination should destroy any sympathy or credibility she might have with the jury.

Judge: "Mr. Morton, I get your drift but I'm warning you. Stop trying to intimidate the witness with such irrelevant remarks and get on with your cross-examination."

Morton: "Certainly, Your Honor. Now Mrs. Roper, referring to your earlier testimony on direct examination, you said that on May 18 you went to Mr. Calcote's home to clean, that he was not there and that you went into the house and began the cleaning. He came home intoxicated and started an argument with you. Is that correct?"

Witness: "Yeah, but that ain't all of it!"

Morton: "Tell us the rest of it."

Witness: "He was pretty drunk and started raisin' hell 'cause he claimed I owed him money for workin' on my ole car. Then he said 'you dint pay me my money, so I'm gonna take it out in trade.' Then he slapped me down and started tearin' off my clothes. I tried to get away and he knocked me down agin. After that he yanked off his pants and raped me!"

Morton: "Well, come on now, Mrs. Roper, isn't the real truth that you consented to intercourse? Really now, at least didn't you just lay back and enjoy it?"

This was the beginning of Morton at his best—an adventure in the art of defensive cross-examination. As his questioning exploded with such audacity his expression exhibited cruelty and his voice became a series of loud booms. Inexperienced witnesses sometimes wilted.

This witness, Ann Roper, seemed to be more combative than timid, however.

Witness: "Hell no, I dint jest lay back and enjoy it! And I shore dint consent to it!"

Morton: "Will you deny that you actually lived, at least part time as man and wife with Marvin Calcote?"

Morton was bearing down.

Witness: "I shore dint live with him like no man and wife!"

Morton: "Knowing that you are under oath, will you deny that you ever willingly had sexual intercourse with Marvin Calcote?"

Witness: "I hate to admit it but I did let him have it a few times. But I shore dint let him have it this here time! He flat raped me!"

Morton: "Come now Mrs. Roper! Do you think for one moment that this fine jury of responsible people will vote to send a man to the gallows who merely continued an er—uh—social relationship that included sexual relations with a woman whom he had generally lived with?"

Witness: "Ain't there a difference when a woman says 'no' and when she says 'yes?' I shore dint say 'yes' that time!"

Morton: "Now Mrs. Roper, let's get into just what kind of person you have been. In other words, have you ever been arrested for any crime?"

Witness: "I don't have to answer that."

Judge: "Mrs. Roper, when you are on the witness stand you must answer that kind of question. That is, about your record."

Witness: "Well, Your Honor, 'scusin' the first three times, I only been up twic't."

Laughter filled the courtroom.

Morton: "Your Honor I insist that you require this witness to come clean with her criminal record and to explain exactly what she means by 'excusing the first three times,' if in fact she has actually been indicted or tried five times. In all my experience, I know of no witness that could dismiss a criminal record by making such a statement."

Judge: "Mrs. Roper, you must explain in detail, exactly what each of the five charges you have implied amount to."

Witness: "Well, what I meant was, I was arrested for not paying for some stuff I got at a department store on two of them times. The other time I was busted for a bad check. The judge made me pay for the stuff I got at the department store and a fifty dollar fine. The other time, I made up the bad check."

Judge: "Mrs. Roper, those offenses cannot be excused. Now, will you please explain the other two cases."

Witness: "Do I have to tell that?"

Judge: "Yes, you do. There is a strong possibility that the defense counsel may have the police report that reveals your conviction anyway."

Witness: "It was when I was young. I was in love with a guy who robbed places and hid the stuff in my apartment. The police got him and they busted me for having stolen stuff on my place. I got five years' probation and he got ten years. I hope you're satisfied, making me tell that!"

Judge: "Thank you, Mrs. Roper, now please tell us about the other case."

Witness: "The other one was 'cause I was workin' at a place that was payin' me under the table, and I was drawin' unemployment money. I only did it 'cause the man I was workin' for was hidin' his money from the state. Then when I was tried, the SOB testified against me. They gave me 90 days."

Judge: "This court is recessed until 2:00 p.m."

The court reconvened at 2:00 p.m.

Judge: "Mr. Morton, you may continue your cross-examination of this witness."

Morton: "Thank you, Your Honor. Now Mrs. Roper I ask you, when Mr. Calcote assaulted you, did he use a weapon and threaten your life if you didn't submit? Did he use a knife or a gun?"

Witness: "Naw, he dint do that."

Morton: "Mrs. Roper, do you consider yourself a physically strong woman?"

Witness: "I guess so, why?"

Morton: "Well, tell us how tall you are and about how much you weigh."

Witness: "I don't know why you need to know that but I'm 5'7" and weigh about 150 pounds."

Morton: "Are you telling this court that Marvin Calcote actually physically overcame you without a weapon, tore off your clothes while you were resisting and was able to penetrate your vagina in spite of your resistance?"

Witness: "He shore did."

Morton: "Were you so terrified that you were physically paralyzed and couldn't move your body?"

Witness: "Naw, I wasn't. I fought against him."

Morton: "Now Mrs. Roper, this is difficult to believe. It seems that in the absence of a weapon and in the absence of threats causing you to be submissive for fear of your life, it comes down to one thing. We would have to believe that he could neutralize all your members—both your legs, both your arms, your upper members such as your neck and head—and prevent a motion of your lower body, specifically your pelvic area that was the critical portion of your body that was his target, to the extent that he could penetrate you. This is incredible, especially when we are aware that my client is only slightly larger in height and weight than you are."

Witness: "I don't care what you say with them fancy words. He flat raped me."

Morton: "Mrs. Roper, I'm going to give you a chance to prove to the jury that your claim of helplessness is believable if you will cooperate."

Witness: "Go ahead with your tricks."

Morton opened his old briefcase and took out an empty eight ounce soda pop bottle. He walked up to the witness chair, very close to the witness, holding the bottle in a horizontal position. He rotated the bottle in a continuous circle with the small opening of the bottle pointed at Ann Roper.

Morton: "Now Mrs. Roper, I want you to try your best to stick your finger into the mouth of this bottle!"

Ann Roper, by this time as nervous as a whore in Sunday School, tried desperately to put an outstretched finger into the bottle without success.

Craning their necks, the spectators began disturbing the order of the court. Having endured the formality and boredom of routine courtroom proceedings, they were now being rewarded with the spectacular performance of the great Hobart Morton. Deputies were instructed by the judge to restore order by evicting several spectators.

The judge recessed court until the following morning.

When the trial resumed the following morning, Judge Phillips, obviously disturbed by the course of the trial thus far, addressed the court.

Judge: "Ladies and gentlemen it is my duty to uphold the law in every respect, to see that justice is done, that all those on trial enjoy the rights that they are guaranteed under our constitution. I feel I have conducted this trial accordingly, but because of certain emotions and related circumstances this trial has bordered on becoming a side-show.

"The defense attorney is a famous and colorful lawyer, entitled to defend his client in any way possible within the bounds of the law and accepted legal ethics. His tactics are not designed to entertain people but to properly defend his client.

"Therefore, during the remainder of this trial there will be no further 'o-o-ohs' and 'a-a-ahs' or other interference with these proceedings. Anyone violating this instruction will be held in contempt of court and jailed until this trial is over."

Attorney Morton's cross-examination continued with no additional intrigue. His shocking demonstration was a complete success. The few remaining witnesses afforded no excitement and appeared to be academic.

Attorney Morton provided no witnesses for the defense. After his devastating cross examination of Ann Roper, he was confident that he could convince the jury to go his way with his forthcoming address to the jury.

After the prosecution and defense had rested their cases, the judge declared a recess until the following day, at which time both sides would make their closing statements to the jury.

The following day at 10:00 a.m. closing statements began. In reality these statements are a sales pitch to the jury by the prosecutor and defense.

The prosecutor went first. He skillfully reviewed his evidence point by point as he walked back and forth in front of the jury. He had serious doubts as to winning the case in view of the background and character of Ann Roper, the alleged victim. His greatest worry, however, was the possibility of the stunning impact Morton's closing argument would have on the jury.

Prosecutor: "Ladies and gentlemen of the jury, it's up to you. You've heard the evidence against the defendant. You've heard the testimony of Ann Roper. But—you have not heard any evidence from the defense.

"Now Mr. Morton will tell you that a person cannot be compelled to testify against himself. That is one of the rights guaranteed to every citizen. That, of course, includes this defendant.

"When you retire to the jury room to reach a verdict, ask yourself why. Why would a lady like Mrs. Roper make up a false story against any man when she has nothing to gain?

"Also please ask yourself why the defendant chose not to testify, even though as I said, he couldn't be compelled to do so.

"But, ladies and gentlemen there is no law in this land to prohibit him from voluntarily testifying. And why shouldn't he, if he is innocent?

"My most important words to you however, are to inform you that the counsel for the defense, being one of the most successful criminal lawyers in this country, is cunning and will amaze you! A small example you have already seen during the cross-examination of Ann Roper!

"Mr. Morton will do his best to inject sufficient doubt about the guilt of his client into your minds. And his best is incredible.

"So, please remember this! Do not let his tricks sway you! Thank you. This concludes my closing statement."

Judge: "The court will take a 30 minute recess."

While the trial was in recess, Morton guided his client to a small study room adjacent to the courtroom for a secret conference.

"Marvin, when we return to court, your guilt or innocence—literally your life or death—depends on the kind of job I do with the jury. You have got to weep! I mean you must cry your heart out. This will cause the jury to think you are a sentimental, humble and remorseful soul. Can you turn on the tears when you want to?"

"I don't think I can," replied Calcote. "The last time I cried was when a guy kicked me in the balls. That was several years ago."

"That's what I was afraid of," said Morton. "Now, I've got something here that will make you look humble and remorseful."

The lawyer took an object wrapped in wax paper from his briefcase. He unwrapped a large onion, cut in half.

"Now, soon as I start making my plea to the jury, take this onion without anyone seeing it and rub it on your hands real good. Then rub your eyes with both hands and you will cry whether you want to or not! You got that? This will fit right in with my plea to the jury. Okay?"

Before Calcote could answer, they received word the trial was resuming.

Judge: "Mr. Morton, are you ready to make your closing statement?"

Morton: "First, Your Honor, the defense wishes to make a motion for a direct judgment of not guilty."

Judge: "I will hear your motion. The jury will be excused."

Morton: "Thank you, Your Honor. You may have taken judicial notice that the only witness presented by the prosecution has been discredited, in that she admits having to do with the defendant prior to her claim of rape. We respectfully request a directed verdict of not guilty as to Marvin Calcote."

Judge: "Motion denied, Mr. Morton. Are you ready to issue your closing statement?"

Morton: "Yes, Your Honor."

The jury was recalled. The anxious spectators were on the edge of their seats now that the legendary genius of Hobart Morton was to be exhibited in his summary statement to the jury and for that matter, to the full court!

Morton: "If Your Honor please.

"Ladies and gentlemen of this honorable court! It is a very rare pleasure for a simple country lawyer like myself to be honored by appearing before such an impressive jury as this—men and women who have been selected because of their beauty, intelligence and presumed character—a people who, because of those traits, will see that justice is done. My job therefore is to show you that justice will be completely served only if you find the defendant Marvin Calcote innocent of these charges.

"Now, let me go back to the basics. Ann Roper is a woman who has been arrested several times. Please remember her comment when I asked her if she had been charged with any crime! She testified that, 'Scusin' them first three times, I only been up twic't.'

"She admitted to having certain encounters—in fact, sexual encounters—with the defendant prior to her claim of rape.

"Ladies and gentlemen of the jury, it is my earnest belief that she for some reason became angry with my client, Marvin Calcote. She decided to bring him in here, hoping that through your deliberations you would hang him!

"Ladies and gentlemen of the jury, I must say this. I truly believe that the greatest creation that God Almighty has given us is a good woman! Ann Roper is not a good woman. I will add that the worst creation is a bad woman! Ann Roper is a bad woman! There are a multitude of good women in this world! But there are many bad women such as the witness in this case, Ann Roper.

"As to that minority of bad women, I can only surmise that if they did not have a 'vi-noochie' there would be a substantial bounty on them."

Attorney Morton then called Marvin Calcote to follow him. Placing his arm over Calcote's shoulders, he guided him to the jury box. He could tell that Calcote had followed his instructions about using the onion. Calcote's eyes were watery and tears were already streaking his cheeks.

"Ladies and gentlemen of the jury, and if Your Honor please, look at this simple man who is in tears. He is completely devastated, thinking that he could actually be put to death solely for being acquainted with a female who willingly submitted to many men. It has been reliably reported that this evil woman had sex with fourteen men under Curtis Bridge in one night—!"

At this point Ann Roper jumped up and shouted, "That's a goddamn lie. It won't but eight!"

Morton was elated with her outburst. In effect, she was acknowledging an act that he had no way to prove!

Consequently he eased his rhetoric and began to praise his client. He placed his arm around the defendant and paraded him before the jury. By this time Calcote's tears, brought about by the onion, were very obvious to the jury.

Morton: "Look at this remorseful human being! He is weeping, not because he fears punishment but because he knows in his heart he is innocent.

"I must tell you that I have known this humble man for years!"

By this time Morton was employing all his skills to sway the jury.

Morton: "Ladies and gentlemen of the jury, this great man, a God-fearing Christian, is one of the finest people I have ever known. Why, some great day in the hereafter I expect to walk the marble halls of heaven, dressed in the purple cloaks of eternity with this great man! Set him free! Set him FREE!"

Morton thanked the jury and the judge, concluding his defense.

Marvin Calcote, after weeping profusely before the jury throughout the final argument, slipped into the men's room and discarded the large onion.

The judge declared a recess until the next day.

On the following day, after ruling against several motions, Judge Phillips began his charge to the jury. He went over the rules of evidence and explained the law and how these rules applied to this case. In the early afternoon he instructed them to retire to the jury room to contemplate a verdict.

The jury began deliberations at about 2:00 p.m. At 3:45 p.m. they sent a message to the judge that they had reached a verdict. The judge ordered them back into the courtroom.

The Clerk of Court handed the judge the verdict on a piece of paper. The judge casually unfolded the paper and announced the verdict. "Not guilty."

Hobart Morton had won again. After the crowd had dispersed, Morton approached the judge.

"Well, Judge, now that it's over, let's go have a drink!" Morton exclaimed.

"All right," said Judge Phillips. "Have you still got some of your client's good corn whiskey?"

"Sure, Judge! What the hell do you think he's paying me with?"

"Just what I suspected," said the Judge. "I think what you've been furnishing me to drink for years, comes from your client in this case. But I gotta tell you, although you're my friend you are a real son of a bitch when it comes to defending such assholes as Marvin Calcote."

"Right, Judge! But now that the bastard is free, we can still enjoy this premium stuff he makes. And don't be so cranky. After all, everybody knows you stole the last election."

"Lots of folks think I did," said the Judge. "But the truth is, I didn't steal the election. I bought the goddamn thing and paid for it!"

# ALABAMA OR BUST

He is a graduate of the University of Alabama. For a couple of years of the four that he attended that factory of knowledge, he was one of the tidal waves of the Crimson Tide, the university's famous football squad.

A "speed of light" running back, native Alabamian C. Richard Hearn later migrated to North Carolina under the auspices of the U.S. Treasury Department as a rookie ATF agent.

Initially assigned to the Dunn post of duty in Harnett County, he instantly established himself as an ace investigator and raiding officer, a great morale builder who was funny as a rubber crutch.

Within the territory that was the responsibility of the four man crew was an area about six miles square known as "Broadslab." It was mostly agricultural with many medium size farms sporting very healthy crops such as corn, soybeans and cotton.

The most common utilization of the land, however, was not for crops but for the manufacture of moonshine. Although the distilleries were only medium sized, they were as thick in numbers as a swarm of "dog dick gnats." In fact, stills were much like assholes. Everyone seemed to have one.

When I first met Richard he had been with ATF about one year. During that year he was almost killed by a bootlegging SOB from Broadslab named Webb.

Acting on information he had received, Richard and his leader jumped two men loading several cases of moonshine whiskey into a Cadillac in a remote wooded area. Richard grabbed one of the men standing outside the car.

Experienced violators routinely are prepared to make a quick getaway in case of an emergency. Webb, who was sitting under the steering wheel with the motor running, swung the car door open on the driver's side. The automobile lurched forward knocking Richard down. Webb drove over him, then put the car in reverse and backed over Richard's already badly injured body before jumping out of the car and fleeing on foot into the brush.

How Richard could possibly have done it no one knows—nevertheless he crawled from under the car and apprehended Webb after a chase of several hundred yards. The feat was especially puzzling after medical doctors in an emergency room announced the severity of Richard's injuries, which included many torn muscles and nerves in the spinal area. It can only be assumed that Richard's steely determination and a probable state of shock, combined with his natural abundance of courage enabled such a superhuman effort.

Richard's group leader, M.L. Goodwin, another Alabama native of equal qualities, gave immediate chase to the third violator who had fled into the brush. Manuel apprehended his quarry.

Returning to the scene with his prisoner, M.L. found Richard in extreme agony but still holding Webb, whom he had handcuffed to himself. M.L. radioed other agents who took the prisoners to jail while he rushed Richard to a nearby hospital.

Prior to entering federal law enforcement, M.L. and Richard had both worked as police officers for the Birmingham Police Department. They were two of the very best officers I ever had the pleasure of working with in 25 years of action packed service.

I first met M.L. in 1958 while I was serving as group leader of twelve agents in Wilkes County in the foothills of the Blue Ridge Mountains. Our territory consisted of four counties that were considered the "moonshine capital of the world." It was by far the wildest and woolliest duty that ATF could offer anywhere. Agents assigned there were either the youngest, most athletic men just out of college, or those who had screwed up badly someplace else. In those latter cases it seemed that as punishment, the brass' policy was to "send the bastard to North Wilkesboro and let Joe Carter walk his goddam ass off in those mountains."

This was not the situation with M.L. Most new agents were assigned to an area temporarily to undercover investigations, mostly because they were unknown. This was how I first became acquainted with M.L. I had requested his services for that purpose. He was selected and did a great job. It was his remarkable service over a short period of time that motivated me to later recommend him for the group leader position at the Dunn post of duty, after I became a group supervisor of the seven county area surrounding Raleigh.

Dunn was the second most active post in the state, which itself was the number one state in the U.S. in the manufacture of nontaxpaid whiskey. This is probably the only field where North Carolina has ever reigned as number one.

As area supervisor I took advantage of every opportunity to accompany other agents on raids, especially night raids. It was on such a raid in the Dunn territory that I saw the reality of Richard's physical condition, which was definitely not good. Almost all night raids resulted in injuries, either to violators or raiding officers. Usually this was caused by the violators attempting to escape through the dark woods at breakneck speed. Often when the agent overtakes the violator he must subdue him physically.

On this occasion, about a year after being run over by the Cadillac, Richard caught a violator fleeing from a whiskey still after an exhaustive chase. The man put up a fight but was overcome by Richard, who immediately became desperately ill. He turned white from shock and began vomiting violently. We took him to a nearby hospital emergency room. It seemed that he was well known there. Privately I inquired of M.L. as to the frequency of these occurrences.

"Every time he is involved in this type of action," was M.L.'s reply.

"Do you mean to tell me that this guy has to suffer like this just to do his job?"

In reference to the term "group leader" I am glad to say that the word "boss" was never used by those above me, nor by me to those under me. I was very fortunate to find it unnecessary to consider a single man whom I was responsible for supervising as anything but a friend, peer, comrade or otherwise an equal. I believe that the secret to such an ongoing relationship is establishing a strong mutual respect and by a leader being—well, a leader—who is willing not only to share in the inevitable dangers and other hardships but also to "go first."

Both of these young Alabamians were strongly of this nature, and eventually went on to higher leadership in the organization. M.L. rose to national prominence. Richard served as a leader in two areas but was forced to retire early due to his injuries.

Richard's sheer guts and love for his job made a strong and lasting impression on me. My admiration for him grew as I came to know him. He was always upbeat in his attitude and was the funniest human being I have ever known. It was almost impossible for any of his associates to stay "down in the dumps" in Richard's presence.

And how he loved Alabama! He loved everything about it, most especially its beautiful women and the legendary Bear Bryant, head coach of the "Crimson Tide."

Richard campaigned fiercely at every opportunity with any and all persons who might have influence with management, to hustle a transfer to the state of Alabama. It was a near obsession, which became somewhat of a standing but good-natured joke. When teased about his good fortune of living and working in wonderful North Carolina instead of a "second rate" state such as Alabama, he responded that if he owned a home in Carolina and a farm in hell, he would sell his home and go back to the farm.

As Richard's supervisor I tried various ways to shield him from as much physical activity as possible in the hope that he would recover completely from the near fatal injuries he sustained during the arrest of Webb. However, when action appeared to be imminent there was no stopping him. To try would have been as futile as sending a one-legged man to a "country ass kicking!" Give him information on the location and probable time of operation of a moonshine still and he was as eager as an escaped convict in a whorehouse with a credit card.

When M.L. was promoted and transferred to another state, I recommended Richard for the leadership position at the Dunn post. This was designed to keep him in the office on administrative work so he would have less exposure to the physical combat with violators. It was a very good idea. There was only one thing wrong as was the case with many of my brilliant ideas. It didn't work.

After a couple of years of living in constant pain, still gung-ho and still so active that he had no chance to completely recover from his injuries, Richard was transferred to the big office in Charlotte to serve as leader of field operations. This too was supposed to keep him almost entirely in the office on paperwork. He did an excellent job on administrative functions, but that was primarily daytime work. There still were the nights in which he continued his hard-charging campaign against violators of federal law.

In spite of his incredible courage and dedication, Richard finally realized he should retire. After setting a record of sorts in the Western Judicial District of North Carolina, he requested and received a disability retirement. Needless to say, he retired to his hometown of Jasper, Alabama.

Richard remains a good friend. If he possesses an attribute more admirable than his courage and determination, it is his upbeat personality and sense of humor.

I cherish the memories of a multitude of incidents of real pleasure and fun during my relationship with this character.

On one occasion while we were lying on a still waiting for some activity, Richard took out a copy of a hilarious letter, which by the shielded light of a flashlight he insisted that I read. The letter was obviously a creation of his imagination but nevertheless quite entertaining:

Possum Gulch, Arkansas
October 10, 1929

Credit Manager

Sears Roebuck & Co.

Memphis, Tennessee

Just received your super-heated letter in an open
envelope with a one cent stamp on it, and it would have
given me and the boys much more pleasure and amuse-
ment had not the melancholy reflection come with it
that there were bastards in these United States with the
guts to dun a decent American citizen with an open
letter and a one cent stamp on it.

You stated that you thought the bill should have
been paid a long time ago, and that you couldn't understand why it wasn't. Well, I will enlighten you.

In 1907, I bought a small saw mill on credit, then
came a cyclone and blew the damn thing all over the
next county. In 1909, I bought an ox team, a timber cart,
two Texas ponies, a breach loading shot-gun, a wire
tester, and a $25 Colt revolver; also two fine Razorback
hogs, and all on the damned installment plan. In 1910,
lightning struck my barn, killed both oxen, burned the
barn, (including the timber cart), and those wild damn
ponies nearly trampled me to death in a manure pile
when I tried to save them from burning to death. One
of them fell through my well box, caved the well in, and
carried a new rope and well bucket with him. The other
one ran through my neighbor's garden and was filled
with buckshot. The very next night, (as if I hadn't had
enough trouble) I tried to shoot some damn chicken

thieves with the shotgun, but there was a dirt-dauber's next packed in the barrel and it exploded in my face. I lost a good upper plate, one eye, and what had been my good looks. One of the boys thought the wire tester was a crowbar and broke it in four pieces trying to prize a six-by-six loose from the neighbor's wagon bridge (the one that shot my pony). My oldest boy got drunk and tried to shoot up the town with the pistol and was arrested. It took the pistol and $41 to get him out, then some dirty bastard stole both of my hogs while I was in town trying to get my boy out of jail.

In 1911, my father died and my brother was lynched for horse stealing. A railroader knocked up my daughter and I had to pay a doctor $88 to keep the little bastard from becoming a relative of mine. In 1914, one of my boys got the mumps and they went down on him and the doctor had to castrate him to save his life. Then I went fishing and the boat turned over; I lost the biggest catfish I ever saw, and two of my boys drowned (neither being the one that was castrated).

In 1926, my wife ran off with a heavy hung nigger and left me with a pair of twins as souvenirs. Then I married the hired girl to keep expenses down, but I had trouble getting her to come off. I went to the doctor and he advised me to create some kind of excitement about the time I thought she was ready. That night I took a shotgun to bed with me and when I thought she was ready, I stuck the shotgun out the window and fired. I ruptured myself, my wife shit in the bed, and I shot the best damn cow I ever had. Then some dirty bastard denutted my best bull.

In 1927, I took heart again and bought a manure spreader, a Deering binder, and a John Deere tractor—all on credit. Two months later a tornado struck and blew them all away, including my new barn, a new wagon, and a loft full of hay and feed. My house lost its top and one of the boys had his nuts ripped out by a flying plank with a nail in it. Then I took to heavy drinking and I didn't stop until all I had left was a Waterbury watch and a stricture. Then for some time I kept busy, winding my watch and running to piss.

My wife caught the clap from a traveling salesman and my youngest son wiped his ass on a corn cob that had rat poison on it and had to have half of his ass-hole cut out.

I decided it was time to move, so we packed up and took a train for Texas. On the way one of the twins lost the train tickets and the other shit in the lady's lap that was holding him. She slapped him and he spit in her face, then she started bawling. The conductor tried to throw me off the train for molesting women. Then my son (the rat poison victim) pulled the emergency cord and the stupid engineer wrecked the train trying to stop on a bad curve, nearly killing all of us. At present, I'm awaiting trial for molesting a woman, wrecking a train, and beating hell out of a conductor. If it cost a nickel to take a shit, I'd have to vomit and be satisfied.

Nothing surprised me more than when you said you could cause me trouble, for if you see where I've missed anything, for Christ's sake dig in, for trying to get money out of me would be like trying to poke melted butter up a wildcat's ass with a hot awl. Sue and be damned—you're welcome to try.

Yours for more credit,

Silas Hardluck

# Joseph E. Carter

When in the company of Richard Hearn, it was unlikely that one would be bored, depressed, or suffer from low morale.

Another humorous event concerning Richard arose out of an incident in which I was involved.

I met my supervisor from Atlanta, Mr. John Corbin, one of the best human beings on earth; Assistant Supervisor in Charge Joe Folger and Special Investigator Owen Bean for a journey from Raleigh to Bryson City in the very mountainous far western portion of the state. Our mission was to further the investigation of certain federal law violations reportedly involving several interstate racketeers. Mr. Corbin was a native of the Blue Ridge mountains near Asheville. His family owned a summer resort-type cabin in a vast and remote area. As our working day was anticipated to conclude near the cabin, we planned to spend the first night there, relaxing with some booze (tax paid) which we had purchased in Asheville.

By the time we reached the cabin, it had begun raining, making it necessary to place Mr. Corbin's barbecue grill inside the cabin fireplace. After cooking our steaks and drinking our booze we decided to have a game of friendship, better known as poker.

Although all these men were friends whom I had known for a long time, I had not been closely associated with Mr. Folger, due to the fact that he had been stationed a long distance from the areas where I had served. He had been promoted only recently to the position of Assistant Supervisor in Charge of all enforcement operations for ATF in the state, with the exception of those few of us who were assigned to

158

what I have always referred to as the "racketeering squad."

It has always been beneficial to have this kind of mission with a variety of associates to forge even closer working relationships, and to "get to know" each other better.

As a result of this mission, we certainly got to know Mr. Folger in a way we would not have liked. He had been a group leader at New Bern, an excellent Special Investigator, and for a while an Area Supervisor in eastern North Carolina. This assignment was brief as he was soon promoted to the number two executive position. He was widely recognized as a very good investigator, a very likable and able supervisor.

I had noticed that he consumed much more than his "portion" of the bourbon during the meal, but thought nothing of that until we got into the poker game. As the game progressed, he kept visiting another room which was to be his bedroom for the night. When he returned to the table he was noticeably more "out of it." He became very argumentative and hostile. He verbally abused each person present, challenging each of us to actually fight. His conduct was mostly ignored until he took a large knife from his pocket and stuck it into the table. I took the knife and threw it out of a window and escorted him to his bed.

All during the night I heard him moving around and talking to himself. At one point he came into the living room, went over to the fireplace where the barbecue grill was still located, and proceeded to piss in the grill, thinking it was a bathroom commode.

The following morning we had to change our travel plans as he was still roaring drunk. He had obviously been drinking all night. Completely out of control, he had to be forcibly removed from the auto-mobile driver's position, insisting that he was going to drive.

Totally out of character for Mr. Folger, that incident was very sad and disturbing to everyone who knew him. We assumed that his new elevated position of responsibility as the second in command over sixty agents and the large staff of administrative personnel was probably too much to cope with. As a result of this tragic experience, Mr. Folger was eventually demoted and transferred to the state of ALABAMA!

I could not resist relating the story to Richard. His immediate comment was, "Well I'll be damned. I've been kissing every ass I could reach, hoping and praying that I could brown-nose my way back home to Alabama, when all I would have had to do was piss in the boss's barbecue grill!"

Richard and I have maintained a solid friendship in all the years since our retirement. I have visited him and his lovely wife Sue many times. I recall one of my first visits to their home. A family from Alabama was visiting them. He introduced the visiting lady as his former wife, Doris, and her husband as his "husband in law." What a relationship! His former wife and her current husband were week-long guests in his home!

The one big obstacle to sustained harmony in Richard and Sue's marriage is the annual football game between Alabama and Auburn—a conflict in which "no prisoners are taken." Like Richard, Sue is a native Alabamian—but unlike him, she is a graduate of Auburn.

Sue is a lovely lady, a school teacher of renown with an agenda of family values. She has concentrated her efforts towards educating and training children from birth to develop into productive and responsible citizens.

Like all other wives of ATF agents her task was difficult. Most of the family responsibilities fell to her because Richard was never at home. In those years ATF's primary task in the South was to assure the enforcement of the U.S. liquor laws—a serious tax problem.

There were no rules concerning the time of day or night an agent would be called to work. The violators and the weather determined the time of the activity. Neither of them had any inclination to set a schedule desirable to the agents. On the contrary, if there was an option the violators would operate at a time *not* suitable for investigating agents!

As an ATF wife Sue had long tolerated these conditions—like most others, she did an admirable job. However, the annual battle between the University of Alabama and Auburn served to suspend all marital responsibilities between Sue and Richard for almost a month!

Not being a graduate of *any* university (I have always said, the only college I was ever close to is Pfeiffer on my way to the liquor store), I was not usually up to date on the world of sports events. But whenever I arrived at Richard's house, I knew instinctively when

Alabama-Auburn fever had infected this normally Christian home.

Being radically loyal to the Alabama Crimson Tide, Richard usually was the victor in their war, as the Tide normally defeated Auburn. The always positive and comical Richard enjoyed needling Sue to the point of making her angry. He derived great pleasure in rubbing it in.

In fun I usually attempted to assist Sue.

"Richard," I'd say, "I'm very reluctant to be the bearer of sad news but I just heard a radio bulletin that coach Bear Bryant is in the hospital in critical condition. He suffered a terrible accident this morning. He was enjoying a weekend on the lake, walking on water when a motorboat ran over him!"

Richard was not impressed. "Dammit, Joe, you pulled that shit on me two years ago!"

All this was among friends.

Richard said, "I ain't never smoked a cigarette in my life, but Sue is a former chain smoker. She claims she has quit smoking. It's real hard for me to believe, even though I haven't seen her smoke for over a month. I think she's slipping and smoking, though."

"If you haven't seen her do it, Buddy, how can you say that?" I asked.

"Because I've seen the nicotine stains in her drawers," he responded.

At that remark, Sue called him a name that did not compliment his parentage.

Faking anger, Richard said, "If you want to fight, Darling, strip to the waist and come out swinging!"

During another one of my visits, Sue became upset with Richard for flirting with other women—grandmothers, mothers, wives, daughters, *et al.*, age notwithstanding. I encouraged her not to take him seriously as he was merely full of life.

"Yeah, but he's more full of something else," she complained. "He burns me up! He was born with just one ball, and he goes up and down the street pinching every female he sees on the ass or hugging and kissing them, and in my presence! He acts like he's got a bucket full of balls!

Richard has such a radiant personality that I sometimes believe he could piss on the front steps of City Hall at high noon and receive a certificate of meritorious service from the Mayor, for the act.

There is almost no end to our list of adventures together, bonding two people in friendship through very dangerous missions, long hours, exposure to all the natural elements and physical, emotional and legal risks.

The temptation to write of a few of these experiences was irresistible.

# THE KIDNAPPERS

Gus Gainey was a man with a heart—a good businessman who owned and operated an all night restaurant located in the edge of Wilmington, North Carolina, a coastal city with U.S. highways serving travelers throughout the eastern part of the nation.

Gus's place was never closed, day or night, Sundays or holidays. A famous motto hung overhead in blue neon lights: "We doze but never close."

Gus and his family lived in a large house behind the restaurant for many years. The property lay near the edge of a southern county notorious for bootlegging whiskey. Many of its citizens were poor and uneducated.

As a result, the barons of the illegal alcohol manufacturing racket found a ready and willing work force of unlimited proportions to do their dirty work, at minimum wages.

Gus Gainey, by virtue of his living there all of his life, and because of his operating such a popular place, knew most everyone within miles. He was charitable to the populace in many ways, especially when they were arrested by U.S. Treasury agents at "moonshine" distilleries.

Prior to my advent on the scene, and prior to my acquaintance and friendship with Gus Gainey, the poor bastards were dragged before the U.S. Commissioner, who at that time was appointed to his position because he was a ward-heeling politician, by a higher ward-heeling politician (a *much* higher politician) who was an appointed federal judge, (the best job in the U.S.)

In all my experience at other posts, a defendant provided one bond when arraigned, which covered his arrest arraignment and his preliminary hearing. This bond was always $500. Usually a relative or friend would sign the bond, which cost him nothing.

In Wilmington, the center of the seven county area of the state that was my responsibility, all defendants were taken before the appropriate official, who forthwith called a certain son of a bitch, the only licensed bondsman in the area, who mercilessly overcharged and doubled up on fees for signing bonds. The poor (usually uneducated Black) man was required to pay 10% of his arraignment bond, which amounted to $50 and the following day he had to pay an additional $50 for his hearing bond—a corrupt double dealing practice by that certain SOB, aided and abetted by the U.S. Commissioner.

Gus Gainey and I had become good friends. I made him aware of the injustice being suffered by so many people and suggested that he obtain a license as a bondsman and assured him that by charging fees that were fair, he would be doing a good service to the community.

This he did. He signed the bonds at no charge to the poor unfortunates. Naturally this infuriated the other so-called bondsman as it cut off a major source of his income.

In desperation he bought a penny postcard (in those days there was such an unbelievable thing as a one-cent postcard), and wrote on it, "The chief agent of ATF, namely Joe E. Carter is a racketeer in cahoots with Gus Gainey, in the bonding business and the sugar business (sugar was a necessary ingredient in the manufacture of illicit whiskey) and is believed to be a member of the KKK."

This enormous investment was mailed by the bondsman, a balding fat ass little Jew, to the U.S. Government headhunters, officially known as inspectors or Internal Affairs agents but unofficially known by real, working field agents by other names, some of which reflected quite adversely on their parentage.

The allegations, authored by a man with the morals of a tumble turd who invested the staggering sum of one cent, caused a "Red Alert" in the plush offices of the United States Headhunters. The *head* headhunter lost little time in assigning an agent to jump on this threat to the national security!

Several thousand dollars must have been budgeted for this important investigation.

I base this estimate on the fact that it took the headhunter agent over two years to question a majority of the population of the U.S. in a futile effort to pry loose any evidence of imperfection in my behavior and manner of executing and carrying out my responsibilities as a moonshine "revenooer."

Having failed to do so, he found himself face to face with a dilemma. If he could only find me (he frequently searched where I recently had been) he would ask me to take the oath and make an affidavit by truthfully answering his questions. Undoubtedly he was praying that I might confess to something, even though it might only be something like this:

Headhunter: "Now Investigator Carter, did you or did you not, enter ATF on *Tuesday*, April 25?"

Carter: "Yes sir, I did."

Headhunter: "Ah-ha. I knew I'd nail you. April 25 was on *Monday*! You are under oath, so now we'll have you indicted for perjury!"

And that particular headhunter graduated from the headhunter academy, head of the class. Number 2 of 2300!

The above skit is hypothetical. When I finally met with him, I was placed under oath and questioned as follows:

Him: "Mr. Carter, while stationed in Wilmington, North Carolina, did you know a bondsman by the name of Frystein?"

Me: "Yes, I did."

Him: "Well, did you have trouble with him?"

Me: "Everyone had trouble with him."

Him: "Well, did you call him a son of a bitch?"

Me: "No, sir, not exactly."

Him: "Remember now, you are under oath."

Me: "Yeah, I know. You asked me to tell the *whole* truth."

Him: "Then, just exactly what did you call him?"

Me: "I called him a goddamn, mother fucking, lying son of a bitch."

Him: "He also claimed that you were wearing a side-arm at the time, and that he was afraid that you might use it on him. Is that true?"

Me: "I remember him saying something about my revolver and not wanting it used on him. I told him not to worry, that I would never shoot him, mainly because I wouldn't waste a 30 cent bullet on such a bad investment—but that I might make him eat it, or else stick it up his fat ass if he continued telling such lies on Gus and me."

Him: "What else happened?"

Me: "Nothing. Except for what I've just said, it was a warm, cordial meeting. Effective, too. I believe at least the son of a bitch has ceased trying to assassinate the impeccable character of two such Christian gentlemen as Gus Gainey and me. Oh, I did tell him that I thought he would crawl over 100 whores to fuck his dying mother."

In the meantime, I did a mini-investigation of Mr. Frystein. My inquiry revealed that he had been convicted some years before in U.S. District Court for tax evasion, a felony. When I revealed this to the agent who questioned me his reaction was, "I don't want to hear about him. *You* are the subject of my investigation." (A national hero, like me?)

Mr. Frystein was most likely the Jewish merchant I heard about in a humorous story:

The merchant operated a pawn shop and bonding business. At the time he and his wife and baby lived two doors down the street from his office. Each day she would prepare a luncheon for him and take the infant with her to his office to allow him to go home and enjoy his meal.

On one occasion, she was minding the store while Frystein was home eating lunch. Suddenly she burst into the house in panic.

"Abe! Abe! she shouted. "The store is on fire! The baby's in the store! Get the baby!"

"To *hell* with the baby, get the cash-a-register!" was his response.

After Gus Gainey toppled the corrupt practice of Frystein, his new business of posting bonds for his neighbors/customers invariably caused him some headaches. On one occasion he posted a large bond for a defendant involved in a serious crime, who "took a powder." That is to say, he "hauled ass" to New York City.

Not realizing that the laws of the state of North Carolina were not necessarily compatible with those of the state of New York, Gus asked two agents who were part of my crew to go to New York and bring the fugitive back to North Carolina, so as to be relieved of forking over two grand.

In North Carolina a bondsman responsible for the appearance of a defendant in court has authority to apprehend the bondee and turn him over to the authorities. Thus they are relieved of their responsibility for the appearance in court of the bondee for the trial.

But North Carolina state law is not New York state law. The two agents were eager to go after the fugitive. Gus had promised to award each of them $250 and to pay for all expenses of the trip, including the thirty or forty cases of beer he knew they would consume.

Orville and Chester jumped at the offer. They requested and were authorized a week's annual leave. Armed with money from Gus and the suspected address of the fugitive in New York, they hit the trail.

This was great! A paid trip to the Big Apple and seven days relief from the hard time imposed on them by "Joltin' Joe" Carter, which would have meant fifteen- to eighteen-hour days of hardship.

Orville and Chester, driving one of Gus's cars, stopped at a Baltimore bar, deciding to reward themselves with some relaxation after the stress and responsibilities of such an important mission.

While enjoying the atmosphere and hospitality of the bar, they observed a large red-headed female, probably 2 1/2 ax handles wide at the ass, who was obviously already half inebriated, enter the bar with a large, white domesticated goose under her arm.

A patron, himself three sheets in the wind, said, "What you doing in here with that pig?"

The woman replied, "This ain't a pig, you bastard, this is a goose!"

"I was talking to the goddamn goose!" stated the drunk.

According to Orville and Chester, in my de-briefing of them when they returned, while enjoying a Manhattan in another bar in New Jersey they observed another drinking female. She came into the bar very upset and in a shrill voice cried, "Boy, am I pissed. I just got a fuckin' speeding ticket!"

A bar patron, barely able to sit upright on his bar stool said, "Well, lady, how fast was you fuckin'?"

Chester and Orville continued their journey to New York City and found the fugitive at the address provided by Gus. Unfortunately for the agents, he was Black, a former sharecropper from eastern North Carolina. He was a mild person, non-violent, homesick and eager to be taken back South. He was a typical victim of southern discrimination and very humble about his dilemma, happy to have a free ride home.

The fugitive actually drove the car while Chester and Orville assaulted the supply of beer throughout the pleasant journey South.

Both agents, highly trained and knowledgeable in the ways of most criminals, were relaxed and unconcerned about any violence.

Upon their arrival back in North Carolina, the fugitive was turned over to local authorities, thereby saving Gus from forfeiting his bond.

The two traveling agents reported for duty the following day in rare and happy form. "How was the trip?" I asked them.

"G-r-r-eat!" replied Chester. "Just can't wait for another opportunity to visit New York."

"You won't have to wait long," I told them. "I just had a call from our big boss, and there are two New York police officers on the way down here now with felony warrants for the both of you and for Gus. He will get to go with you this time, 'cause they have one for him, too."

"Bullshit, Joe, warrants for what?" Orville asked.

"Kidnapping. You know, the Black bond jumper, Cletus Tyson, that drove you two drunks home from New York."

"But hell, Joe, ole Cletus is just a good old southern guy who didn't like the Black dudes in New York, or anything else about that big place. He was homesick and actually begged us to give him a ride home," whined Chester.

"You guys do not realize the gravity of the situation. You see, this is another example of the diversity of, well, everything as relates to those above and below the Mason/Dixon line."

"As you know, those Yankees are for motherhood, apple pie, the flag and civil rights. As to civil rights, they insist on Blacks and whites integrating in the South, but not so in some areas of the North. Take Boston for example. The problem is primarily because of the politicians, and it's not right. The prima-donna politicians jump on the civil rights agenda, both white and Black, and use it to their advantage."

"So, now you bastards have got ATF on the spot. But whatever you do, don't waive your rights, especially concerning extradition. If you do, those Yankee bastards will hang your ass. Watch your steps closely. Don't do any of your usual wild stuff and don't bother to try to evade arrest. Just retain the best attorney you can find and be prepared to post a helluva big bond. And, by the way, cross your fingers, pray a lot and keep a tight asshole, because this is very serious."

On occasion, I have seen serious physical and emotional effects resulting from such trauma as a dangerous close call during the execution of a raid, a tight-rope undercover assignment, the death of a suspect or agent, even an urgent telephone call from a surreptitious girl friend who says, "I didn't want to worry you until I was sure, but I am three weeks past due"—such problems as severe weight loss, insomnia, high blood pressure and locked bowels (sometimes locked wide open.) It is not generally true, however, that these direct job problems cause us to abuse alcohol. Usually, we have long ago begun to abuse alcohol anyway, mostly because of indirect job problems such as our bosses and all of those unnecessary government reports.

But none of ATF's crises, ordeals or other phenomena had such an impact on the particular subjects as the "kidnapping" arrests of Chester and Orville. Throughout this ordeal, the two agents suffered weight loss, sleeplessness and were generally as nervous as a whore in Sunday School.

During the following six months, hard efforts were made to resolve the problem for Chester and Orville.

Such efforts included diplomatic liaison by local police, SBI and more importantly by brilliant elderly criminal lawyers who had served for many years as prosecuting attorneys for the Superior Court of North Carolina. Both agents were so well liked by so many people that we were able to keep it out of the news media. This of course was considered a near miracle and required the cooperation of the two agents from New York who delivered the warrants.

Ultimately, Chester and Orville got off the hook through all our efforts, but not Gus. Although he was able to evade service of the warrant, for the rest of his life the New York state felony warrant was outstanding against him, making him a fugitive from New York justice. The New York warrant was never served on Gus, however, mainly because he was killed in an auto accident soon after the kidnapping episode.

The problem still ensues for ATF. It was sure to be an issue used as a weapon in the ongoing efforts by the constant parade of high-level bureaucratic SOB's who are always trying to liquidate ATF as an enforcement agency.

In the beginning, this was to be a simple shortcut to justice, but as it turned out, it was very much the long way around.

# THE LYNCHING OF ALEC WHITLEY

Temple Whitley was in a quite serious frame of mind as he stalked towards Christian Burris. He was of the opinion that since his sister Susanna had borne Christian's children, the least Christian could do was make Susanna his wife. After a lengthy one-sided discussion, Christian agreed with Temple that marriage was probably in order and invited his would-be brother-in-law home with him while he changed his clothes for the ceremony. Temple took a seat on Christian's front porch, impatiently waiting while Christian supposedly dressed for the wedding. When the reluctant bridegroom did not reappear, Temple walked around to the rear of the house. He was just in time to catch a glimpse of Christian fleeing in the distance.

At what point the irate brother intervened in the romance between his sister and her lover is unclear. The affair, which lasted for a number of years, produced four children. One offspring, Rufus Whitley, was a Confederate soldier. Alexander, who was probably the youngest, was not born until 1861, the year the Civil War began. It was Alexander, or Alec as he came to be called, who was the most tragic product of this adulterous union and perhaps one of the most notorious figures in Stanly County history.

Little is known of Alec Whitley's childhood except that he was raised primarily by his mother. He grew to be a fairly large man and is said to have been rather handsome. As he approached maturity, fighting and drinking became two of his favorite pastimes. He also enjoyed stealing, especially from farmers in the western part of the county.

On at least two occasions Alec visited his first cousin, Israel Whitley, for the purpose of stealing chickens. The two had been at odds for some time. In fact, Israel's wife Omie Jane feared Alec so much that she persuaded Israel to move to Catawba County. But Israel, not one to be cowered, bought a double-barrel shotgun and returned to Stanly County, letting it be known that he intended to stay. One evening after dusk Alec visited his cousin's farm with chicken stealing on his mind. He was foiled in his attempt when Israel's dog began barking. Making his retreat, Alec rewarded the guardian's alertness with a bullet but only grazed the dog's skull.

To guard against a recurrence of such activity and to allow Israel the rest he needed for his daily farm chores, Omie Jane stayed awake nights with the loaded shotgun anticipating another visit from the unwelcome relative. She punched a hole in the mud chinking between the logs of their home so she could observe the wounded dog tied to a stake in the yard.

A night or two later Alec returned to complete his mission.

Omie Jane knew of previous canine trouble between Alec and Israel's mother Annie. One day as Alec walked along the road in front of Annie's house, apparently minding his own business, her dog began barking. Annie's dog was not as lucky as Israel's. That time the bullet found its mark.

When Annie appeared on her front porch and shouted at Alec, he shot at her, too. Luckily she was not harmed but her front door did not fare as well.

On Tuesday morning, March 20, 1883, Alec appeared in Concord before the Cabarrus County Superior Court with his brother Rufus and his brother-in-law Philip "Bud" Cagle. They were there because the home of a Mr. Smith, a resident of the southern part of Cabarrus County, had been burglarized. Suspicion pointed toward Alec, Bud Cagle and other parties of Stanly County. The next morning the grand jury delivered two bills of indictment for larceny against Alec and one against Rufus.

Christian Burris was on hand and stood bond for his two sons. Although Alec had two counts of larceny against him, his bond was only $200 while Rufus's was set at $500, suggesting the grand jury had stronger evidence against the latter. Rufus was eventually acquitted of all charges. Alec was convicted, but for reasons not stated in the court records the judge granted him a new trial and raised his bond to $300.

On March 20, 1885, the grand jury brought another indictment for larceny against Alec. On April 26, 1886, Alec failed to appear in court as ordered. He was absent until May 2, 1887, at which time the court dismissed the case with leave, keeping open the possibility that he could be tried later. It is not clear why Alec was absent for over a year, but his excuse was evidently satisfactory since Christian Burris did not have to forfeit the bond he had posted.

Bud Cagle turned state's evidence in the Smith burglary case and was ordered to appear in court again on September 19, 1883 to answer separate charges of fighting with one John Hinson. He failed to do so and remained absent until November 2, 1885, at which time his case was dismissed with leave.

Not only were Alec and Cagle in court at Concord, but at the same time they were also involved in judicial proceedings in Albemarle. On March 30, 1883, the Stanly County Superior Court delivered two bills of indictment against Cagle, one for "burning a house," the other for larceny. There is no record of conviction on either indictment, but Alec and his wife Mary (Cagle's sister) are listed as witnesses in both cases. Whether they were witnesses for the state or for the defense is not mentioned.

About a year prior to this, Alec and Cagle were co-defendants at Albemarle on a charge of affray. The records do not specify whether the two were fighting each other or fighting together in a brawl.

Suddenly, Bud Cagle was nowhere to be found. *The Stanly News* suggests that he never returned to the courtroom in Concord after his trouble with John Hinson. This is obviously false. A Charlotte newspaper contends Cagle was killed by Alec and others involved in the Smith burglary. The latter possibility cannot be ruled out. Perhaps the two incidents in

Albemarle, combined with the fact that Cagle was a state's witness in Concord, generated ill will between them. However, according to court records, Cagle's second appearance in the Concord courtroom came *after* Alec's first trial and *before* the second trial at which Alec's case was dismissed with leave. This would suggest that although Cagle was a state's witness, he apparently gave little or no damaging testimony against Alec.

The *Stanly News* quotes Alec's cousin George L. Whitley as saying that he took Cagle "over the River Jordan" and gave him fifty cents, and that Cagle would never come back. What George Whitley meant by this Biblical phrase is unclear. On one occasion he supposedly said he took Cagle to "the line," gave him fifty cents and told him never to return. If Whitley did make such a statement, perhaps he was referring to the North Carolina-South Carolina line. This would tend to corroborate a claim made by Alec just before he was hanged that Cagle was living in South Carolina. A search of a rock quarry where he was believed buried produced no signs of his body. To this day Bud Cagle's fate remains a mystery.

Regardless of the circumstances surrounding Cagle's disappearance, Alec and his half-sister Judy Burris later left Stanly County and traveled to Arkansas. They eventually settled near Arkadelphia in Clark County and lived together as man and wife. Alec began using Burris as his surname and some news accounts of the day refer to Judy as "Mrs. Burris," but it is doubtful the pair ever married. Shortly thereafter a Stanly County schoolteacher by the name of Burt

Tucker made the journey to Arkansas—a journey which cost him his life.

There are several contradictory accounts of Tucker being killed. According to Judy Burris, he visited her and Alec frequently. On one of these occasions Alec and Tucker made a trip into nearby Arkadelphia and did not return until late that evening. They had been drinking and were in the midst of a quarrel by the time they reached Alec's home. Several times Tucker remarked to Alec, "You don't confidence what I say to you."

After the quarrel Tucker left and went to a neighbor's house. Shortly afterwards the neighbor's young son came to Alec and asked him to come and get Tucker. Alec did as the boy asked, carrying a heavy stick with him. As they were returning to Alec's home, Alec struck Tucker with the stick. The blow evidently disabled Tucker.

Sandy Wilson, a man who had been working for Alec, assisted Alec in bringing Tucker inside. After a few minutes the two men helped Tucker, whose head and face were bleeding, into an adjoining room and put him to bed.

Around two o'clock in the morning, Tucker got out of bed under his own power and left Alec's house. At daybreak Alec also left, not telling Judy where he was going. Sometime later he returned, told her Tucker was dead, and threatened harm to her if she said anything about the recent events. Afterwards, Wilson and Alec placed Tucker's body in a room of Alec's house and covered the corpse.

At this point Alec considered turning himself in to the sheriff, but Wilson persuaded him not to, saying he would put Tucker away. While Alec held a gun on Judy, Wilson dismembered the dead man's body. Later, the two men put Tucker's remains in sacks and threw them in a creek.

*The Stanly News* gives a somewhat different version of Tucker's death. According to this news article the two were playing cards when an argument developed. Alec claimed Tucker drew a pistol and he hit Tucker in the head in self defense. The article goes on to say Tucker's throat was cut just above the collar, although it fails to say who did the cutting. Later Alec and Wilson (his first name is given as "Sam" in this account) carved the body into several pieces, boxed up the gory cargo, and put the box in a creek.

The above account speculates that robbery was also a motive for the killing. Furthermore, during the argument Tucker supposedly threatened to expose Alec in a previous killing and Alec wanted to silence the schoolteacher.

One old newspaper claims Alec had sworn several years earlier during an argument that he would someday kill Tucker. It is possible, and some contend quite probable, that both men had romantic notions concerning Judy and that jealousy was at least a contributing factor, if not the primary cause of the quarrel.

Discrepancies as to the date of Tucker's death also exist among the various accounts. Judy claimed the killing occurred on January 24, 1892. *The Stanly News* states it took place almost a month later on February 20. Two Arkansas newspapers place the date in late April, although one reverses itself in the same article and in another article a week later by agreeing with February as the date of death.

Daniel Burton Tucker had been a likable but somewhat controversial character long before he followed Judy and Alec to Arkansas. Behind him remained a wife and several children. A former Republican candidate for sheriff of Stanly County, Tucker had at one time been expelled from the college at Mt. Pleasant for gambling. yet he was known as an able schoolteacher for his day. Considered handsome, he had the reputation of being quite popular with women. He supposedly always carried snuff—not for his own use, but as a courtesy to the fairer sex, since it was fashionable for young ladies of the day to use tobacco in this form. It has been said Burt Tucker had a heart ailment, which could have been a factor in his death.

In addition to being charged with the deaths of Bud Cagle and Burt Tucker, Alec was also accused by one newspaper of killing his wife, Mary Cagle. The article goes on to say that Judy Burris claimed Alec killed his two children while in Arkansas. No mention is made of who the mother of the children was, the ages or sex of the children, or for what reason Alec supposedly slew them.

Local legend denies these sordid accusations. Most people say Mary Cagle died of natural causes and was buried somewhere in Cabarrus County before Alec left for Arkansas. Also, sometime after the lynching, Judy supposedly admitted to one Stanly County woman that she was the mother of the children and said they died of natural causes—not by Alec's hand.

Besides the above alleged crimes, Alec supposedly threatened the lives of several people including John Drye, a deputy sheriff of Stanly County, who was later instrumental in his capture; and Arch Eudy, another of his first cousins.

After the killing, Alec evidently tried to make it appear that Tucker had left Arkadelphia in an attempt to hide the latter's death. He shipped a trunk containing Tucker's belongings to Argenta (now North Little Rock), addressed to D.B. Tucker, then called for and received the trunk himself. He then brought the trunk on to North Carolina by forging the dead man's name on a railroad order. The original bill of lading for the trunk was found on Tucker's remains.

According to Judy Burris, after Alec received Tucker's trunk, the two of them traveled together until they reached Gainesville, Georgia. Once they parted company, she apparently arrived in Stanly County before he did. Sometime during the week prior to the lynching, she was jailed in Albemarle. Previously, Stanly Sheriff Isaac Wilson "Buck" Snuggs had been notified by the Clark County sheriff's office to be on the lookout for the couple. Governor Thomas M. Holt, North Carolina's chief executive at the time, placed a $200 reward on Alec's head.

Alec managed to evade capture until June 6, 1892. On Sunday, June 5, he was seen by the wife of Deputy Sheriff John Drye. Upon learning of this, Drye formed a posse. Its estimated size ranged from 23 to 45 men. Once formed, the posse made its way toward Big Lick to the home of Ephraim I. Whitley, a first cousin of Alec.

The fugitive spent Sunday night in Ephraim's barn. Sometime before dawn, Ephraim's younger son

Obadiah went out to the barn to feed the stock. As he entered the barn, Alec called down from the loft and told him of the posse. Obadiah immediately returned to the house and informed his mother of their visitor. She invited Alec into the house and gave him some breakfast. After he finished eating she allowed him to lie down, but warned that if the posse came he would have to leave—she wanted no shooting there.

Alec had not finished his breakfast before the posse surrounded Ephraim Whitley's house. At daybreak some of the men approached the house from the front. Alec bolted from the rear of the house and ran into an orchard where an officer holding a shotgun ordered him to stop. Alec was immediately searched and relieved of a Derringer, a knife and 30 cents.

After the capture, the posse headed back to Albemarle. Word of Alec's apprehension spread quickly and the lawmen were soon joined by a crowd of excited people. When they reached the home of Israel Whitley, he was asked to drive a wagon and transport some of the people into Albemarle. Somewhere along the way a few of the men wanted to put a rope around Alec's neck in order to force him into a confession of killing Burt Tucker. Israel objected for fear that it would turn into a lynching on the spot, and the idea was forgotten.

When the procession reached Albemarle, Alec was put in jail where he stayed three days. The next day, Tuesday, June 7, Clark County deputy sheriff T. Winn Singleton arrived. Singleton was to wait in Albemarle for Sheriff James Abrahams (pronounced "Abrams") to arrive either Thursday or Friday evening. The two officers would then escort Judy and Alec back to Arkadelphia.

It is possible Abrahams had information on Tucker's death that has since been lost. At least he was confident that Alec would be cleared of the charges against him.

Fearing possible trouble, Sheriff Snuggs had posted a small guard to protect the prisoner. As a mob began forming on the streets of Albemarle, Snuggs summoned several men from throughout the county, whom he felt to be influential, to come and mingle with the crowd. He reasoned that these men discouraging any vigilante actions would be more successful in preventing violence than a show of force by himself and his deputies. It is also said the sheriff moved his other prisoners from the jail to his home across the street (now the Stanly County Historical Museum) to insure their safety.

About two o'clock Thursday morning, June 9, 1892, a mob of around 75 to 100 Stanly and Cabarrus County men appeared at the jail and demanded Alec Whitley. When confronted by the mob, Snuggs' resistance seems to have been limited to pleading with the men and a refusal to give up the keys. When these efforts failed, the mob broke the lock on Alec's cell with an ax and carried him from the jail begging for his life.

A Confederate veteran who had lost a leg at Spotsylvania, Sheriff Snuggs was heavily outnumbered, and doubtless a shootout would have proven futile. However, there seems to be a question as to the desire of some of the law officers to stop the lynchmen. One deputy who was in the jail at the time supposedly said later to a grand jury investigating the lynching, "I couldn't see killing my friends for the likes of Alec Whitley."

James Abrahams arrived in Albemarle sooner than expected, but not soon enough to prevent the miscarriage of justice. The Arkansas sheriff followed the mob to Town Creek Grove with the hope of being able to cut Alec down before he died. When the mob reached its destination, a rope was thrown over the limb of a red oak tree. Alec was set astride a gray mule and a hangman's noose was placed around his neck. Alec confessed to none of the charges against him. He did say that Burt Tucker was killed in his (Alec's) house, but claimed some man named Goodman, who was never found, committed the deed. He also claimed that Bud Cagle was living in South Carolina and asked the mob to give him three days to produce his missing brother-in-law.

At this point someone asked the mob to pause so the condemned man could make peace with his Maker. After a few moments of silence, the mule was spirited away. One of the lynchmen leaped up and embraced Alec's body to add his own weight to the suspension. Another even mounted the dying man's shoulders in order to hasten death.

He hung there in full view of passers-by until sometime that evening when the coroner came to examine the body. The results of the inquest were sealed and sent to Clark County, Arkansas. After the inquest, a grave was dug for Alec beneath the tree where he was lynched. There is some doubt, though, that he was ever buried there. In 1927 the grave was opened and little was found. There were only two bones that looked like the upper leg bones of a cow. A Dr. Talley, who viewed the remains, said the bones resembled human bones, although he never actually said they were human bones. There was also a blue suit rolled up as if someone had dropped it into the grave—not stretched out as if it had been on a corpse. The suit looked intact and the color was still good, but when touched it crumbled very easily. Most of those present shared the opinion that Alec never rested in the grave under the red oak tree.

What was found in the grave was placed in a pine box and taken to the cemetery at Smith's Grove Primitive Church near Oakboro. Later a monument was erected with the following inscription:

ALEXANDER

WHITLEY

SEPT. 15, 1861

JUNE 10, 1894

NOT OUR WILL, BUT THINE

BE DONE.

On Friday, June 10, 1892 Sheriff Abrahams and Deputy Singleton left Albemarle with Judy to return to

Clark County, Arkansas, where she would answer the charge of complicity in the death of Burt Tucker. The bills of indictment against her and George L. Whitley, who earlier had also moved to Arkansas and was also charged in connection with Tucker's killing, were endorsed "ignored" and they were released by the County Circuit Court on August 18, 1892. After being cleared, Judy came back to Stanly County. Sometime later she moved to South Carolina where she spent the rest of a long life.

George Whitley's alleged involvement in Tucker's death had been looked into as early as May of 1892, During an "examining trial" the state produced a witness against Whitley named Joseph Hall from Dalark in neighboring Dallas County. On the 24th of May Hall was discharged from the case and went to Hope in Hempstead County to visit his mother. After a few days in Hope he boarded a train to return to Dalark and subsequently disappeared. He was still missing on June 17. It has been suggested, although no proof was given, that Hall's disappearance was linked to his testimony against George Whitley.

Some speculate that Sandy or Sam Wilson came to Stanly County after Tucker's death and that he might have participated in the lynching. If he did come, more than likely he didn't stay long. No one knows for sure whatever became of him.

Probably no one has ever claimed that J. Alexander Whitley was a good man. Yet, there are those who do contend he was no worse than many of the men who acted as his judge and jury in the early hours of that June morning. It is not inconceivable that some of his executioners wanted Alec dead to prevent him from embarrassing them in court. On the other hand, Alec Whitley was genuinely feared by many people in Stanly County and there was some feeling that he would never have reached the gallows had he been returned to Arkansas. Even this, of course, does not excuse the actions of the lynchmen. They denied him many rights guaranteed by law.

In a sense though, it is somewhat presumptuous for anyone today to attempt to judge either Alec Whitley or the vigilantes. Being a generation or two removed, there is no way to appreciate fully the human emotions of participants on either side of the tragedy. They have all been gone for many years and no doubt have taken many secrets to their graves.

Whether or not he was guilty of the crimes charged against him is something that will most likely never be known for sure. The whole truth about Bud Cagle, Burt Tucker, and the other alleged murders will probably never come to light. It has all been obscured by the lynching of Alec Whitley.

*Arkadelphia Herald*

**Arkadelphia, Arkansas**

**Friday, August 26, 1892**

## JUDY BURRIS' STATEMENT

After Judy Burris had been set free by the court she was permitted by her attorney to make any statement that she desired touching the Tucker murder. A *Herald* man sought an interview with her at Mrs. Mackey's boarding house where she and her father were stopping. She consented willingly to the interview, and was found not averse to making a full and free statement of the facts and circumstances connected with the brutal murder of D.B. Tucker as far as she knew them. Her statement was—

My name is Judy Burris. My home is in Stanly County, N.C. I am 22 years old. I came out from North Carolina with Alex Whitley, alias Burris nearly four years ago. We lived in this county two years. Tucker and Whitley claimed to be cousins. Tucker had a wife and four or five children in North Carolina. He came to Arkansas something more than a year ago now. He was in the habit of visiting Alec Whitley at our house previous to the killing which occurred on Saturday night, January 23rd, last. Tucker came over on Thursday, January 21st, previous to the killing. They both went to Arkadelphia Saturday and came home late. I heard them coming, and heard Tucker say, "you don't confidence what I say to you" and continued making that remark after they came into the house. They were drinking. After their quarrel Tucker left and went over to Marion Anderson's. Shortly afterwards Mr. Anderson's boy came over and said he wanted Whitley to come and get his man (or friend, I did not understand which.) Alex went after Tucker and carried a heavy stick. On returning with him he struck him with the stick just inside or outside of the gate—I did not see but heard the blow, and did not know whether he knocked him down or not. Sandy Wilson, a man who had been working for Alex about a month or so was there, and they two brought Tucker in the house and placed him in a chair. He did not complain of being hurt, but his head and face were bleeding. After a few minutes Sandy and Alex helped Tucker into an adjoining room and put him to bed. I was so nervous I could not sleep that night. About 2 o'clock Sunday morning I heard Tucker get up and go to the water bucket, then go out of doors. Alex said he supposed Tucker had gone to get something to kill him with. About daybreak Alex got up and went out. I don't know where he went or what he did. He came back after awhile and told me Tucker was dead, and, taking his pistol, said he would kill me if I made any alarm. He would not let me go out. They put Tucker in a little room and covered him up. Alex spoke of coming to town and giving up to the sheriff, but Sandy said no—said he would put Tucker away—that he had put many a man away safely. About 12 o'clock Sunday, Alex took his pistol and guarded me while Sandy went into the little room and cut up the body of Tucker. About 12 o'clock Sunday night they put the remains in sacks and carried them to a creek a half mile away and dumped them into the water they said. We left that place about five weeks after the killing. We left Sandy in Little Rock and I never heard of him afterwards. Alex and I went to Memphis and there to Covington, and thence to Detroit, Tenn., where my father sent me money to come home on. Alex Whitley traveled with me as far as Gainesville, Ga. There he said that he thought it best to never let me go home, but I begged till he consented and he told me that if I ever told anything he would hunt me up and kill me. I never saw Whitley after we parted.

**The *Stanly News***

**Albemarle, N.C.**

**Thursday, June 9, 1892**

## A HORRIBLE MURDER

---

Alex. Whitley Kills Burt Tucker.

— Escapes. — Captured and Lynched in this County.

---

Died Denying all Charges.

Searching For Cagle's Remains.

Near Arkadelphia, Ark., on Saturday, the 20th day of February, last, was the scene of one of the most horrible and cruel crimes we have ever heard of—perpetrated by for-mer citizens of this county upon another citizen.

Two years ago, D.B. Tucker left this county for Arkansas. His deportment in that country made him many friends, and he was held in high respect.

Two years before Tucker's moving west, Alex Whitley, a desperate character of this county, ran away with Judy Burris, his half sister, accompanied by his cousins George and Green Whitley. Alex Whitley changed his name to Burris, and he and his half sister lived together as man and wife. Whitley, or Burris, as he was known there, was feared by all who knew him—not for his boldness but for his sneaking and underhanded tricks.

Burris, George Whitley and Tucker had to appear at Little Rock, Ark. Superior Court, as witnesses in a certain case. Of the three, Burris was the only one who appeared. Officers were sent in quest of Tucker and Whitley. The latter was found and summoned. On being asked where Tucker was,

192

he burst into crying and said that Tucker had been killed by Burris. Whitley related in full the confession Burris had recently made to him, which we give in substance:

Burris, when asked by Whitley where Tucker was, replied, "I killed him. Tucker and I were playing cards and he won several dollars from me. He drew a pistol on me and I struck him on the head with a cudgel and knocked him down." He made it appear that he did this in self defense. Tucker's throat was then cut just above the collar; he was then placed upon a bed and covered up until Sunday morning when one Sam Wilson, with Burris and his wife, carved the body into several pieces, cutting head and limbs from the body; on Sunday night they boxed the pieces up and secreted them in a creek near by, where they were found by a Negro, two months afterwards.

It is thought that Burris had, a short time before, killed another person, and that Tucker was the only other person who knew it; and when the quarrel arose, Tucker threatened to expose Burris, and the latter decided to make way with him. Another supposition is that Tucker had considerable money and that Burris sought to get it.

Burris made his escape to this county and was captured on last Monday morning at the residence of M.A. Whitley, a J.P., of Big Lick Township. He and Judy Burris both repose in jail here awaiting the coming of the sheriff of Clark County, Ark., who is expected this or tomorrow evening.

Mr. T.W. Singleton, deputy sheriff of Clark County, Ark., arrived Tuesday with proper papers from Gov. Holt for the removal of Judy Burris to Ark.

The case has created great excitement, and circumstances are woven so closely together that not a single loophole exists for Alex Whitley's (Burris') escape.

George Whitley is now in jail in Arkansas, and efforts are being made to capture Wilson, who is thought to be in this county.

Whitley denies killing Tucker and told us that he had not seen him since last January. He says he is not a bit uneasy, and feels confident that he will come clear.

———————

Some six years ago, on Sunday morning, a robbery was committed in the southern part of Cabarrus County and suspicion pointed toward one Philip Cagle, Alex Whitley and other parties of Stanly County. Search was made and the property was found and identified by a Mr. Smith, whose house had been broken into. Arrests were made immediately and the trial came off at Concord. Cagle turned States evidence against Alex Whitley and others, and it looked as if they could not escape justice; but Cagle got into a difficulty in Concord, struck Peg-Leg John Hinson on the head with a rock and ran away. it is said the he went to the house of Alex Whitley, his brother-in-law, who harbored him. George L.

Whitley told it that he took Cagle over the River Jordan, gave him 50 cents, and that he left and would never come back. Others said that foul means had been used and that Cagle had been killed and concealed in a rock quarry on the lands of Alex Whitley. Later circumstances seem to point to the latter supposition, and men are today searching the premises and quarry for the body of Cagle. Next week, we will give further information if any discoveries are made.

———————

## The Lynching

A mob composed of 75 or 100 Stanly and Cabarrus County men stormed the jail about 2 o'clock this morning and demanded of Sheriff Snuggs the keys to Alex Whitley's cell. The Sheriff said, "You may take them by force, but I'll never give them up." They forced an entrance into the jail by means of an ax and broke the shackles that bound

Whitley. Whitley cried, prayed, plead with the men; Dr. Anderson, Sheriff Snuggs and others besought them to let justice take its course, and pointed to them the attending dangers; but the disguised bloody shirt men, armed to the teeth, paid no heed—nothing but Whitley would satisfy them. About 150 yards from Town Creek bridge, they swung him to the limb of a tree, where he now hangs, a ghastly sight, waiting the coming of the coroner. He said to the last he was not guilty and did not confess to other crimes charged against him. He said Philip Cagle is now living in South Carolina.

It is, indeed, a pitiful sight. We regret that space does not admit of minute mention.

**The *Daily Standard***

**Concord, N.C.**

**Thursday, June 9, 1892**

# STANLY HAS A

# LYNCHING

---

**Alex Whitley, or Burris,**

**Swung to a Tree**

---

Masked Men Break Into Albemarle's Jail And Take Alex Whitley Out And Swing Him to a Tree—The Sheriff Overpowered—He Makes No Confessions.

Special to *The Standard.*

Albemarle, N.C., June 9.

At 1:30 o'clock this morning a band of masked and disfigured men (about 75 in number), appeared at the jail here and demanded prisoner Alexander Whitley. Sheriff Snuggs had a small guard on the lookout for the mob, fears of lynching being entertained by some.

The men came with bloody shirts on, and fully determined to have Whitley or shed blood in the attempt to get him.

The mob demanded the keys of Sheriff Snuggs. He stood his ground bravely and held on to the keys. Failing to get the keys, the mob broke through all the doors, reached Whitley, cut the shackles, secured the prisoner and hastened off to the west side of Albemarle across the creek which borders the town, and there swung him to the limb of a tree.

Whitley plead innocent and made no confession to any other crimes, but he said that Tucker was killed in his (Whitley's) house in Arkadelphia, Ark., but by another party.

Everything passed off quietly and Whitley's lifeless body hangs in the breeze this morning. J.D.B.

---

Whitley stood charged with the murder of D.B. Tucker sometime in February last, the deed being committed in Arkansas. This is the first murder, by lynching, ever committed in Stanly. It is a genuine sensation.

That mob has done wrong if law be right. They stand today guilty of a crime that is more heinous than the one with which Whitley was charged. But in this day when justice miscarries and our courts fail to do their duty, there is no surprise at some people taking the law in their own hands.

Both Whitley and Tucker were Stanly born men. Tucker attended school at the college at Mt. Pleasant, and while known as a bright and intellectual man, he was considered a man of bad character, and when it was known that he was gambling, Tucker was expelled from college. He was one time considered the best public schoolteacher in Stanly, but his association was such as to bring him into evil repute. This Whitley has never been conspicuous for noble deeds.

## Daily *Charlotte Observer*

### Charlotte, N. C.

### Friday, June 10, 1892

LYNCH LAW AT ALBE-MARLE

---

Whitley, the Arkansas Murderer, Swung up by a Mob

---

Details of the Crime for Which He Was Put to Death—The Murder of Burton Tucker in Arkansas

Special to the *Observer.*

CONCORD, N.C., June 9. – On the 20th of February there occurred in Arkansas one of the bloodiest murders on record. Mr. D. Burton Tucker, for many years lived in Stanly County and was somewhat of a Republican politician there; in fact he was a candidate for sheriff at one time. He went to Arkansas to live. While there he was foully murdered. He, it is stated, had both arms and both legs and his head cut off on said night. Mr. Alex Whitley was with Tucker on the night of the murder, and was not seen in Arkansas after that time. Whitley formerly lived in Stanly County also. It is thought that the two men were playing cards and that Whitley killed Tucker for his money. After this report was out, a sharp lookout was made in Stanly, suspecting that he might return to his old home. A reward of $200 was placed on his head by the Governor. Last Sunday a woman named Dry saw him pass near her door.

She told her husband and he collected a posse of men, and they followed his trail. They surrounded the house of Ephraim Whitley, a justice of peace, and found Alex Whitley locked up in one room therein. Ephraim Whitley is a relative of the suspect man, and he was in Albemarle a few days before and asked why they did not search for him, while at the same time he was shielding him at home from the law. Whitley, seeing himself surrounded by an armed mob, bolted from the door and attempted to escape by running. But Mr. John Dry obstructed his way with a loaded gun, and commanded him to throw up his hands or he would shoot him. This he did. Then Arch Eudy and twenty-two other men bound him and took him to Albemarle Monday and placed him in jail. He will be taken to Arkansas to answer the charges against him. It was feared that he would be severely dealt with by this determined band of men, but the law will take its course here, but after he reaches Arkansas, and if the charge is true, it is doubt-ful whether he will reach a lawful death or not. Nothing of late years has so excited our neighbor county as this affair. Everybody almost was eager that the suspected murderer should be brought to justice. Alex Whitley has a very bad reputation, and is considered a dangerous man. It was thought that he was interested in another murder a few years ago in Stanly County. Tucker's reputation was not the best, but he was not considered a dangerous character by his countrymen.

This information was procured from persons who know the locality well and who have these facts from several of their friends there. It is thought that Whitley had a partner in this affair who is also lurking somewhere in Stanly.

---

The Murderer Taken from Jail and Hanged Just Outside of Town.

Special to the *Observer.*

SALISBURY, N.C., June 9. – The murderer, Alex

Whitley, alias Burris, who was jailed at Albemarle Monday on a charge of murdering D.B. Tucker, at Arkadelphia, Ark., last February, was lynched early this morning. A mob broke into the jail about two o'clock and secured Whitley and swung him to a tree just outside the town limits.

The keys were demanded of Sheriff Snuggs, but he replied, "You may take them by force, but I'll never give them up." A small guard had been stationed at the jail but it was insufficient to prevent the bloody mob from their work. They came prepared for a struggle in case of resistance. The mob was composed of some 75 or 100 Stanly and Cabarrus County men. They immediately dispersed after the lynching. Great excitement prevails at Albemarle over the transaction. Tucker, the murdered man, and Whitley were both Stanly County men. The Sheriff of Clark County is expected at Albemarle today. He will remove Judy Burris, the alleged wife of Whitley, to Arkadelphia, Ark., for trial on a charge of complicity in the murder.

Whitley made no confession, claiming to the end that he was innocent, but said that Tucker was killed in his house.

**Semi Weekly *Charlotte Observer***

**Charlotte, N. C.**

**Monday, June 13, 1892**

AN AWFUL RECORD OF CRIME

---

Whitley, the Lynched Murderer

---

Said to have Been the Murderer of Five People—Lynched Not so Much on Account of the Tucker Murder as for Former ones.

Special to the *Observer*.

CONCORD, N. C., June 10, 1892. – Everybody is discussing the Whitley-Tucker affair in Stanly county. Nothing in fiction can equal this affair, when everything is considered. It seems Alex Whitley and others, several years ago, stole a lot of money from one Smith. John Cagle knew that these were the guilty parties and in order to get him out of the way they killed him. The courts did not prove this but almost everybody was fully convinced that such was the case. It was supposed that Whitley also killed his first wife. he took her to the mountains and that is the last that was ever seen of her.

The woman named Burris, who was jailed as an accomplice in the Tucker murder since Whitley was lynched, makes some very startling statements. She was afraid of him, and while he was hiding in Stanly she was afraid to leave the house of her father. She says that Whitley, while in Arkansas, killed his two children, and also says that he was the murderer of Tucker.

Whitley, it seems, brought Tucker's trunk here to North Carolina by forging an order on the railroad. Tucker, when found had the bill of lading for it in his pocket, while his trunk was in this state. It is given as a reason for the murder that Whitley had an old grudge at Tucker; besides, they were gambling. Years ago it seems they had a difficulty, and Whitley then said that he would kill him some time.

George Whitley, cousin of the lynched man, is in custody in Arkansas for aiding in this crime. They are a dangerous gang and have been greatly feared by those who know them. The reason this woman did not give him away before he was jailed, was that she knew that Whitley would kill her instantly. This story is not likely to be quite complete, for the Whitleys, it is said, belong to a regular band of cut-throats who no doubt will be heard from further. The Stanly citizens did not lynch Whitley especially for the murder of Tucker, but, they knowing his past record of murder, etc., and seeing that the law did not reach him on those cases, were determined that he should pay the penalty of death—his just desert. Of course, the law should have had its course, but they were afraid that he would, if taken to Arkansas, get away and then more murder would have been the result. And if the woman's story is true, that is that he killed his two innocent children, slew Tucker, mur-dered Cagle and is suspected of killing his first wife, they certainly had some grounds for such action.

These facts were obtained from hearing people converse who live in the locality of the scenes, and are probably true, but I will not vouch for them. Whitley's wife is also his half-sister. It is very probable that she will be released since it is rather evident that she was not an accomplice in the murder.

The facts and information reported herein were obtained by David D. Almond, Jr. through public records, numerous interviews with many individuals and much other exhaustive research.

Permission for its use was generously given by Mr. Almond. His cooperation is graciously acknowledged.

Mr. Almond is an insurance executive in Albemarle, North Carolina. His narrative was copyrighted in 1978, Copyright Registration Number TXU-5062.

Complete and detailed copies may be purchased from Mr. Almond by writing him at 115 Wilson Street, Albemarle or by calling 704-983-1611.

Mr. Almond's excellent narrative includes commentaries by many newspapers on the lynching of Alec Whitley, some of which are incorporated herein. It is interesting to note the difference in the manner of reporting news over 100 years ago from that of today.

After his death a number of ballads about Alec Whitley became popular. Most of them were communicated orally and have long since been forgotten. Fortunately, one by the Rev. Edmond P. Harrington was put in print and has survived.

## SONG BALLAD

lines written on the assassination of

## D. B. Tucker

Come young man of the present age, and listen to my call,

And don't be overtaken by strong alcohol.

There was a man both young and gay, his name to you I'll tell,

It was Burton Tucker, of whom you know so well.

*Chorus*

They dumped him in the water,

The fish swam o'er his breast,

The water in gentle motion,

We hope his soul's at rest.

Times were financially hard, and money coming slow,

He went to the West where many young men go.

He went to his employment, which was teaching school,

His scholars they all loved him, and all obeyed his rules.

He only taught eight months instead of teaching ten,

When he met Aleck Whitley, who brought him to his end.

Yes, he met with Aleck Whitley, all in a smile you see,

"Go home with me Cousin Burton, and get your lodging free."


And after long persuading with him did agree.

He went along home with him where murder was to be.

Aleck says to Wilson, "We've got him now you see,

We will take his life and his money will ours be."


Yes, Aleck watched him close to see that he was not seen.

He raised the fatal weapon and the blood ran down in a stream.

Judy said to Aleck, "Don't this take the lead."

They took him in the back room and laid him on the cotton seed.


The like in old Arkansas had never yet been seen,

They cut his body in pieces, the number seventeen.

Aleck says to Judy, "This secret you must keep."

They cut his body in pieces and dumped it in the creek.


Judy says, "Oh, Aleck, you'll die in public sure,

For murdering Cousin Burton, and mangling his body so.

You'll be arrested for this, and in the jail you'll go.

And on the fatal hangman's tree, you'll pay the debt you owe."


His wife in North Carolina she could not take her rest.

She felt that there was trouble with her husband in the West.

Oftimes she had looked for him, and oftimes seen him come,

But now he is gone from her to never more return.


—Composed by Rev. E. P. Harrington

# THE SECRET EXECUTION

"Joe, grab a flight out of Raleigh and be in Atlanta tomorrow. We have a very special mission for you. Prepare to be gone about a week."

That long-distance voice was my boss, M.L. Goodwin, a rising young government executive with whom I had a great relationship. Naturally, I agreed. M.L. knew me, my tactics and motivation well.

My initial reaction was apprehension, then curiosity. When the big office beckons suddenly, you wonder. What sin or shortcut shenanigan was catching up with me? Where had I failed to cover my tracks? Had I left a loose end dangling to incriminate me? Maybe M.L. had me lined up for some simple investigative assignment—like murder, for instance.

On the plane, my thoughts turned to M.L. and my association with him. He was a handsome bachelor of about thirty, very cool. Women brazenly chased after him in the little city near Raleigh where he had previously been stationed. But somehow he escaped the whirlpool of matrimony. He had a great sense of humor and made no one unhappy except the many unsuccessful women who had permanent designs on him, and of course the multitude of bootleggers he caught.

Not the least among his superlatives was that of "bank runner." This status is usually assigned to a boy in a group of youngsters who gather at some swimming hole in the summer to play naked in the water. Throughout life, the male is judged by the size, specifically the length, of his male organ. The champion of the group is soon recognized at the swimming hole. He gets out of the water and runs around on the bank to show off. The other boys, feeling inferior, remain in the water to their waists. M.L. was awarded the title after a showing, not at a swimming hole, but in the showers at Maxwell Air Force Base in Montgomery, Alabama while we were there on riot duty in the spring of 1963.

M.L. welcomed me into his Atlanta office with a grin and a handshake. "How's everything in the Raleigh area?" he asked.

I knew he was asking about the little brunette doll whose heart he had broken when he moved to Atlanta. M.L. had a close call with her. She was a wealthy tobacco queen who worshipped the ground on which he walked.

"She was doing fine the last time I saw her, M.L. But she must have really given up on you. She married some runny nosed kid about ten years younger."

His grin disappeared momentarily.

He gave me a desk and dumped a stack of folders on it that two tall men couldn't shake hands over.

"This," he said, "is a thirty-five year old murder case. The victim was a federal agent, charged with enforcement of the liquor laws. Throughout the years, it has been assigned to the better agents in SIS in the hope that someone will solve it. Now it's your turn. I know it's a big order and time has made it even more difficult. But the Big Chief in Washington wants us to close the damn thing."

I spent a week at that desk reading the case files and progress reports on the old case. The solution to this case was not to determine the killer. That was already known. Rather, it was to find him. So I considered it a fugitive case.

In the early morning of September 20, 1931, Victor Blythe and Stewart Hall, two federal prohibition agents, slipped through the woods to an illegal distillery in one of the great swamps in Eastern North Carolina. Deep in the swampland, the distillery had been found on a prior visit by Blythe and Hall. Hall had examined the mash and predicted it would be distilled on this date.

From a distance of several hundred yards, Blythe and Hall heard the thrilling sounds of the distillery being operated. Silently they crept over the mossy ground. For over an hour they stalked their quarry, utilizing all their talent and training.

At one hundred and fifty yards they could hear voices. Fifteen minutes' listening convinced them that two men were operating the still. A few minutes more assured them that the operators were the men they suspected and hoped to find. The main one was Solomon Garris, a huge young Black buck of twenty-one who had earned the reputation of being snake-mean and dreaded by law enforcement officers.

How to raid the still? Should one agent circle and approach from the opposite side while the other went straight in? Or should both agents run directly in, taking both operators by surprise? They quickly decided on the latter.

Hall told Blythe, "I'll take Garris, you get the other one."

Cautiously they continued advancing, stopping at fifty yards. They could hope for no more than twenty yards of concealment. It required another ten minutes to cover the final distance to the point where they would rush the operators.

Hall and Blythe glanced at each other. Hall signaled with a jerk of his head. They jumped to their feet and Blythe gave the usual loud yell. Both young and in excellent condition, they quickly covered the distance. Blythe rushed a slender Black who ran like hell. After a short chase, the agent tackled the Negro. He subdued him, handcuffed him, took his wallet to note his name, then started to sit on a log to catch his breath, when he heard a shot.

Pushing his prisoner hurriedly in front of him, Blythe returned to the distillery.

The last breath gurgled through Hall's bloody lips and through a massive hole in his throat. Garris had taken the agent's revolver and killed him with it. He was long gone.

The files, and especially the sworn statement of Blythe, glared these facts. Then came a description of

an unreal search for Garris, beginning with the instan-
taneous pursuit by a rather large posse of officers and
rednecks all through the day and night and into the
next day.

This search led to the home of a friend of Garris,
where he borrowed money and a small rowboat to
cross the river to safety. The friend recalled later in his
affidavit that Garris looked panicky and gave the
impression that he would never be back. Before noon
the next day, the posse wearily returned to town,
telling everyone that they had no luck at all. The files
were loaded with thirty-five years' worth of tips on the
whereabouts of Garris—in New York City, the Baha-
mas, the West Coast and most every other location
where a bored agent might like to take a paid vacation
on Uncle Sam while running down a "lead." The U.S.
Government must have spent hundreds of thousands
on this case from 1931 until the 1960's, mostly on
running down phony tips that led agents to merry,
merry places.

This total effort resulted in exactly nothing. Garris
was never seen or heard from again. As time passed,
witnesses or potential witnesses died one by one.

On my last afternoon before leaving Atlanta, M.L.
and I went out on the town. We had been through a lot
together, both in our work and play, and we had a lot
to talk about.

We laughed again at the time several years earlier
when a North Carolina moonshiner nicknamed Sweet
Mash was found at one of his many stills on a Sunday
morning. M.L. and his crew caught him and destroyed
the still, using up most of the beautiful Sunday morning so engaged, along with fingerprinting and ar-

raigning Sweet Mash. The poor scoundrel was a three-time loser and a cinch to go to prison unless he could get up the money to pay a huge fee to a local attorney who was a drinking buddy of the local judge.

Sweet Mash cursed his luck but said nothing disrespectful to M.L. or his men; not so his wife. Early on Monday morning, a three hundred pound glob of fat, topped by a massive mop of stringy red hair, bombshelled the office routine at ATF headquarters in Raleigh. Of Mrs. Sweet Mash's three hundred pounds, at least one hundred of it was boobs. They wobbled in an orbit of their own within her massive wobble. Never before or since had headquarters taken such a tongue lashing. "Where's the sonofabitch what's in charge of dis chicken shit outfit?" she roared.

M.L. said, "I'm he, Ma'm. What can I do for you?"

"Nothing, you no-good bastard. You've already done too much, ain't you? Done caught Sweet Mash in the hole. Ain't that enough? Don't you know he ain't got a chance not to go to Petersburg? 'Less he can scratch up five thousand dollars for that damn drunk lawyer that gets all the crooks off. I hate for him to even mess with a lawyer that works for crooks, 'cause it hurts his good reputation. I don't know what the hell the world's comin' to. Very idea! The Gov'ment payin' a bunch of fuzzy balled college brats like you and these others, to go out on Sunday, the Lord's day of all times, and catch folks makin' a honest livin.' If you damn sonsofbitches had been in church on Sunday mornin' like you s'pozed to be, my Sweet Mash wouldn't be in dis mess. I ain't never votin' fer another damn one of you agin!"

She waddled out of the office.

M.L. said, "Hear that, boys? If you had been in church like you should have been, Sweet Mash wouldn't be in this mess."

"Gosh, did you see the size of those boobs!" a young agent exclaimed. "I'm sure as hell glad she didn't faint in here. It would have taken six men to take her out—three a-breast."

I told M.L. I suspected that Garris would never be found; that I had read all the material very carefully and believed him dead.

"What makes you think so?" he asked.

"I'm convinced that the posse caught him in the swamp that first night and executed him," I said.

Relaxing on the big jet back to Raleigh, I let my imagination, mind, instinct and experience fill in the pieces of the thirty-five year old baffler. Here's the way I think it ended:

Agent Blythe bent over the body of Hall in terror. "Hall, who did it? Who did it? It was Garris, wasn't it?" He tried for a pulse, finding none. Blythe wasn't completely sure the big Black man had been Garris, but he thought so.

"All right, you nigger bastard," he said, turning menacingly toward his prisoner. "If you don't tell me who it was, the nigger undertaker will drag your dead ass out of here. Tell me now, NOW damn you!" The bore of the .38 along with the click of the hammer quickly convinced the prisoner he had a lot to gain by speaking fast.

"Yah, suh, boss. It was Garris awright. I din't have anything to do with it, honest. Don't kill me, I couldn't hep it."

Blythe forced the prisoner to run in front of him to the car hidden a mile away. They sped to a phone and he called the county sheriff. Then he called his superiors in Baltimore, Maryland. Take charge of the search, he was told. He vowed to get Garris at all costs.

Blythe took his prisoner to jail. At the sheriff's office a large crowd had gathered. The sheriff was on the phone with Central Prison in Raleigh, begging for bloodhounds. Three other federal agents soon arrived.

As was customary, the sheriff selected about a dozen men from the mob of over a hundred and deputized them. "Go home and get your waders, all the high-powered guns and all the ammunition you can carry and be back here in a hurry. The bloodhounds are on the way."

While the men impatiently awaited the arrival of the bloodhounds, Blythe and a crew including the county coroner went out to the scene and brought out the body of Hall. Dynamiting the distillery was deferred until after the chase.

The sheriff was a tough veteran of many years, definitely a non-constitutional type officer as to the fourth and fifth amendments concerning the rights of a citizen about protection against unreasonable search and seizure and the rights of an individual to remain silent when questioned, especially in the case of murder of another officer. To the officer, this is a mortal sin and a suspect has no constitutional rights.

This sheriff had surrounded himself with tough deputies. None looked sharp, but all were tough.

At 1:00 p.m. the bloodhounds arrived from Raleigh, eager to run. They were escorted by a wiry-looking old prison guard and a shifty-eyed trusty.

"How good are they?" asked the sheriff.

"Good 'nuff to bring back what they start after," replied the guard.

"This is one time we don't want to miss," the sheriff said.

He held a fast conference. "Men, I'm in charge of this here hunt. I know these people and I know what to do. All of you, just remember, do as I say and don't ask any damn questions. Whatever happens in here, if anything goes wrong that ain't supposed to, or if anybody comes out and runs his mouth, he answers to me. Y' hear?"

In half a dozen cars, they drove to the still location. The guard asked everyone to stay back while he let his dogs sniff the area, especially some old overalls believed left behind by Garris. Immediately, the dogs took off through the swamp.

The sheriff's plan was to relay his men with the dogs and their escorts, who were accustomed to the torture of trying to keep up with two lunging bloodhounds. Three officers kept in sight or sound of the dogs at all times, changing shifts when the dogs stopped to recover the temporary loss of the trail.

Hour after hour the hunt went laboriously on through the deep swamps. At sundown, the men and dogs came to an edge of the swamp and stopped at an unpainted four room shack. The house faced a rather wide river and sported a wooden boat tied up at the landing. Two of the men went back into the swamp and returned shortly with the sheriff. The sheriff told everyone to take a short walk and leave him alone with Andy, the man of this pitiful household. Andy was an aged Black man known to the sheriff.

"What yo' all lookin' fer, sheriff?"

"Andy, now don't lie to me. Big Garris killed a white officer this morning. You know what that means, Andy? We gonna get him and Lord help anyone who don't cooperate with us. Now I'm going to ask you just once. Didn't Garris come to your house this morning, through here?" He waved an arm at the swamp.

"My goodness, yo' mean Solomon done kilt a white officer? Oh, what we gonna do? Won't nevah be safe no mo' fo' a colored puhson to go to town. Oh me, oh me!" Andy moaned loudly. "Well, I jus' well tell yo' de truth. He come bustin' in heah all right, and he sho' looked wild. He wuz wet all ovah, an' looked scairt to death. He made me give him my money and he borrowed one of my boats. I ast him when he wuz comin' back and bringin' muh boat and money, and he didn't even answer."

The sheriff asked about a gun.

"Didn't see him have one in his hand," Andy said.

The sheriff told Andy he would be back later and he rejoined his posse. He reported the information and instructed the guard with the dogs and two deputies to take Andy's other boat and go across to the nearest landing. If Garris had reached that landing, he could make it on foot through the swamp to a road that led out of the county and to possible safety. The sheriff would take the others back to the cars, then meet them across the river as soon as they could make it to the landing.

The plan called for the party with the dogs to fire one shot if they picked up the trail again, two shots if in hot pursuit, and three shots, continuing at intervals, if Garris were captured.

The sheriff took aside the two deputies to accompany the bloodhounds for a secret conference. He entrusted to them a special mission. "Boys, if we take him in, we may not get him convicted. Nobody is left to testify that they saw him shoot Hall. Andy didn't see no gun. Garris has probably already thrown it away. On top of that, they may not hang the sonofabitch if we do convict him."

He was silent for several minutes, giving his comments time to be considered by the two deputies. He took a long drag on a cigarette and paced back and forth.

"We been working for a long time boys, and we been through a lot. But we ain't never had an officer killed outright before with his killer getting away. I just want to ask you both, and I know that I can trust both o' you or you wouldn't be here. Do we want to take this bastard in and take a chance of him being acquitted, or just getting a prison sentence, or do we want to settle it tonight?" The question was more of a definite statement. "Remember, old Hall was a real friend to us, even if he was a federal officer, and remember his two little boys. They gonna have to grow up without a daddy on account of that bastard."

The deputies looked long and hard at each other, then at the sheriff. "You mean you want us to...?" one asked.

"Yeah, you get the point. I hate to do it or ask you to, but we got to look after justice. You know, some smart lawyer is liable to take his case and frig up the thinkin' of the jury. You know how it is, somebody on a jury might weaken and let the bastard off. Now we just can't have that. If we let some nigger get by with something like this, we'll be at their mercy. Won't be safe for no white woman in the country to walk down the road by herself. And too, if Garris gets off, every nigger in the county will be wantin' to kill an officer. No siree, we just can't have it."

So the pact was made. In the likely event that the dogs caught up with Garris, it was not going to work for the prison guard, the trusty, nor the majority of the posse to see or suspect anything.

"It'll take us an hour to go back to the car and another hour to drive across to the landing. I'll be thinking of some way to get rid of everybody we don't want in on this deal." The sheriff sounded confident.

During the long walk back to the car and the ride to the other side of the river, the sheriff was silently concentrating on whom he could trust and on how to get rid of the others without arousing suspicion. By the time they reached the destination, his plan was made. He turned every contingency over in his mind. This was new. He had spent many years uncovering the evidence to terrible crimes. Now he was about to commit one and he was totally occupied with how to cover it so thoroughly it would never be uncovered.

The rendezvous at the boat landing occurred at midnight. The sheriff saw that part of his plan would be easier than he hoped. Several members of the posse were exhausted. He took advantage of this fact and eliminated many of them by suggesting that a smaller group could go faster with less noise. Several men volunteered to return to town. The sheriff decided to use only his two trusted deputies and of course, Blythe. He didn't like having a federal agent in on the deal, but he had found no way to talk Blythe into giving up the hunt. Blythe and Hall had been very close partners. Too, Blythe would never be able to satisfactorily explain to his superior why he had quit a hot chase for his partner's killer. This didn't worry the sheriff, because he had come to know and respect Blythe quite a lot. He would have to take this chance.

His only remaining concern was how either to keep the prison guard and the trusty from seeing anything, or to seal their mouths forever in the event they did see it. This worry was real. He did not know the guard and the trusty was a criminal who could be expected to do anything in his power to hang an enforcement officer. After all, it probably was an officer who had sent him to prison.

Cutting everyone out except Blythe, his two deputies, the guard and the trusty was easy. He would have to play the rest by ear. He knew that in the hours necessary to overtake Garris he would think of something. Already the final phase of the plan was forming in his mind.

As the team worked with the dogs and again picked up the scent of Garris from Andy's first boat tied at the dock, the sheriff knew what he must do. He joined Blythe and candidly outlined the plan. Blythe bought it without a qualm. He bitterly hated Garris by this time. The death of Hall had hit him hard and he was eager to kill Garris, with his bare hands if necessary.

The sheriff held a group caucus. He assigned two men to go forward with the dogs. He picked the trusty as his partner to work with the dogs. When each two-man team tired, they would stop for the others to catch up and take over the dogs. This was necessary as the powerful dogs covered three times the distance of the men bringing up the rear. They ran and lunged from side to side, temporarily losing the trail and then running back and forth to pick it up again. It was an exhausting job, but the grim thought of the murder and their eagerness to catch the murderer drove them on.

About 2:30 a.m. the sheriff and the prison trusty relieved a deputy and the prison guard with the dogs. By this time, each man in the party had learned the hounds and how to work with them. The trail was getting hotter, indicating that Garris was tiring or was taking longer rest periods. The sheriff knew his quarry was near.

They topped a swell in the ground and left the ankle-deep mud for a moment. The sheriff closed the gap between himself and the trusty, the latter intently watching the dogs. Silently, the sheriff stepped within striking distance and drew his blackjack from a rear pocket. This blow had to be good. With a powerful chop at the base of the skull, he felled the trusty. Quickly he felt for a pulse to assure himself that he had not hit the man too hard. With relief, he found a strong heartbeat. Then he put his handcuffs on the trusty and yelled loudly for the others. His yells continued until they answered.

The prison guard, the deputies and Blythe hurried to the scene. The trusty had partially revived and was able to sit up. His speech had not yet returned. "My Gawd, what the hell's happened?" asked the guard.

"The sonofabitch tried to escape," replied the sheriff. "Why did you bring a damned prisoner that would be likely to run?"

"Damned if he ever did this before," said the guard. "This poor guy was supposed to get paroled next month. Stupid bastard. This means three more years for him, not to mention thirty days in the hole."

Knowing that the guard was instructed never to leave a trusty in the custody of anyone else, the sheriff said, "I'll send the deputies out with him."

"Can't do that, I'd get fired," said the guard. "Ain't no choice but to give up the chase and take him out."

"Give up the chase hell," ripped the sheriff. "No damn way I'll do that. Maybe you can't leave the prisoner but you sure as hell can leave the dogs. We can work them. I'll send one deputy out with you, 'cause I doubt if you would ever find your way out of this mess. But we ain't leaving until we either find Garris or until these hounds can't smell him no more."

The sheriff sounded tough and final. The guard decided he had no choice.

The trusty groaned and began rubbing his head. "What happened?" he mumbled.

"Shut your damned mouth and get off your ass, you no good bastard," the guard shouted.

"I ain't done nothin', I ain't tried to get away," the trusty pleaded. "You all are fixin' to screw up my good time, and I ain't tried to run, I ain't!"

"I said shut your damn mouth," yelled the guard. He kicked the trusty in the rump. "Don't say another word or I'll brain you."

The sheriff sent his eldest deputy with the guard to return the trusty to confinement. He felt a little sick about setting the innocent trusty up for several additional years in prison, but it became necessary for the success of his plan.

"I been thinking this thing out, boys. It sure looks like now that we're going to catch him. We still have a chance to do it right. That is, he may still have the gun and may try to use it. I doubt it. He's probably thrown it away, and if he hasn't, I don't think he has the guts to shoot it out with us. My opinion, he'll give up like a lamb. Anytime there is a killing, you ain't got much of a chance to convict unless there is a corpse. I don't aim for there to be any corpse found, but we can't do but so much to prevent it. If his body is ever found, it is going to have to look like he accidentally drowned. We can't have no bullet holes found in him."

After a ten minute break, the three men loosed the lunging hounds. The trail got hotter all the time. Another hour or so should do it. The grim mission to which the men had committed themselves caused a terrible silence. The biggest sounds were the swamp mud sucking at their feet and the occasional splashing of the dogs through pools. On and on they plunged.

By now the hounds were running less and less from side to side, sticking to a straight line. About 4:00 a.m. both hounds tried desperately to break loose. This meant the quarry was near. A few minutes later they heard sounds of something, or someone, no more than two hundred yards away.

The sheriff yelled, "Garris! Garris! This is the sheriff. You might as well stop and give up. We got you and you ain't got a chance to get away."

"Okay, okay. Don't shoot me! Please don't shoot me! I'm stoppin' right heah!"

Within minutes, the three men were all over Garris. He offered no resistance and reached frantically for the stars.

Handcuffs were thrown on Garris posthaste. Then all four men collapsed on the muddy floor of the dismal swamp. No one in the country could be any more exhausted. All looked like slimy lagoon creatures covered with crusty layers of mud and water.

Garris was terrified. His large brown eyes shone through the mud like those of a wounded deer. He began to realize he would never face a judge for his crime. There was no doubt in his mind as to his fate at the hands of these men. This realization turned his terror into panic. Hysterically, he tried to claw his way to his feet and continue his flight. The lunging of the dogs and the frantic grappling of his captors prevented it.

Then came the tears and the pitiful begging for his life. The officers were not without compassion, but they were determined to carry out their plan. To them, this would be justice, however swift.

The sheriff was reminded by the sight of the straining of the great wrists of Garris against the handcuffs that the final phase of the execution by drowning would be a tough job in spite of the handcuffs and the three-to-one odds. An additional struggle would leave Garris' wrists raw and bleeding. Assuming the body might be found, the sheriff wanted no tell-tale marks. This same reasoning eliminated the easier and somewhat more merciful solution of knocking Garris unconscious with a blackjack prior to drowning him. Cautiously, the sheriff freed Garris' hands, taking a piece of his already tattered shirt and making a cushion around each wrist, then replacing the cuffs.

Garris continued to weep and beg for his life. He swore that Hall had drawn his revolver and hit him with it. An examination of his head revealed no acute bruises from being pistol whipped.

Garris was bluntly informed of what was about to happen to him. He was given the opportunity to say a prayer for his immortal soul. But he only offered a horrible scream which echoed uselessly through the dismal swamp.

Wanting to get the thing over, the sheriff grabbed Garris around the neck and, aided by his deputy and Blythe, committed the terrible act they felt they must. The ordeal took over twenty minutes. A more fierce struggle probably never occurred in the swamp, the shackles on Garris' hands notwithstanding.

Finally, the great body went limp. They held his head under knee deep water for many minutes afterward. Finally, they let go. Blythe checked for a pulse and found none. They were exhausted mentally and physically.

The body could not be left on the open ground. A brief search turned up a suitable hiding place under a hollowed-out bank, out of sight of trappers or hunters who might travel this area. Another thirty minutes of erasing signs of the struggle, dragging and work at the embankment, convinced the three that they had done all they could here.

"I'm lost as hell in this swamp, but I do know that north is that way," pointed the sheriff. "And the nearest road is to the north. The posse will be rested and back riding the roads or on the lookout for us. And we sure as hell don't want nobody coming in here, so let's get the hell out as fast as we can!"

Dawn was an hour old when they departed toward the north, all following the incredible sheriff. The men had been without food and with only swamp water to drink for about twenty-four hours. About mid-morning they could hear the distant sound of automobiles on a road. Such a volume of vehicle traffic was abnormal for this area so they knew that members of the original posse were searching for them. Thirty minutes more of torturous struggle brought them to the road.

Within minutes a deputy drove up in a county car and the men fell on the ground to rest. Questions by the deputy and his rider were unwelcome and this was immediately sensed by the deputy.

Finally, the sheriff said, "The sonofabitch got away. Take us back to town. We'll rest and then carry on from there."

Back at the sheriff's office, most of the members of the posse were on hand, along with a sizable crew of federal agents, some dressed up in suits like they expected to search for Garris on paved streets. Dozens of questions were asked of the sheriff and Blythe. The only response was that Garris had escaped in the swamp, the trail had vanished, and they believed he had made it to the road and was now fleeing the county. This scuttled a plan by members of the waiting group to resume the search in the swamp.

Blythe convinced the federal men that they should take up the search elsewhere, namely on all neighboring farms near the public road, and all villages and towns in that part of the country. The agents bought this suggestion and didn't bother to return to the swamp.

"Let's get cleaned up, get some rest and meet at my place," the sheriff secretly told Blythe and the deputy who had been with them. "We've got some talking to do."

After a long sleep and a good meal, the three met at the home of the sheriff. He sent his wife and daughter to visit neighbors. "Boys, you know what we've done. The way I see it, we ain't done a damn thing wrong, but you know we'll hang if the truth ever comes out. So I'm telling you tonight and I ain't ever going to discuss it with you or anybody else after this. We got to keep our mouths shut forever. No matter how much your conscience works on you, no matter how many bad dreams you have about last night, or how many people question you, we stick to one simple story: Garris got away. He made it to the road and vanished. If either one of you ever talks, it's going to be your ass. Another thing: we can't just stop this search 'cause it won't look right. We got to dig in and work around the clock for a long time, pretending that we are trying to find Garris just to make it look good. 'Cause if we do anything suspicious, they'll go right back in that swamp and they might find the body."

Affidavits indicate this is exactly what the sheriff, Blythe and the others did. A determined search continued in the locality for weeks. Thereafter, investigative reports show that the search continued for the next thirty-five years with no trace of Garris or his body.

When time permitted, I studied and reread the files and came up with an even stronger conviction that I was right. I visited the scene and made a formal effort to contact anyone remaining alive who could possibly be a witness, including members of the posse. All potential witnesses were dead. Blythe was still living but was hopelessly senile and completely incoherent. It was with this information and a medical statement as to Blythe's condition that I returned to Atlanta and reported to M.L. I flatly requested a permanent closing of the case.

While the request was in Washington being considered, Blythe died. A supplemental report including a copy of his death certificate resulted in closing the final page in this long drama.

It is my sincere opinion that these three men succeeded in committing the perfect crime. Nowhere in the massive files, reports, affidavits and sworn statements, nor in the investigation that survived all the potential witnesses, is there the slightest finger of suspicion pointing to them.

Thus, the perfect crime, horrible but true, if my imagination is correct.

# PRESIDENTIAL CONDUCT

One of the agencies in the family of the U.S. Treasury Department is the Secret Service. That agency's chief assignment is one of the most important missions of any law enforcement organization—the personal security of the President of the United States, his family, and others in the service of the nation.

ATF agents are sometimes detailed to assist the Secret Service in their geographical area in protecting the lives of the President, his family, or candidates seeking election to the presidency.

While stationed in Raleigh, North Carolina in the sixties and seventies it was my unfortunate luck to be assigned to accompany several presidents who were visiting the Carolinas. Although such assignments may sound exciting to someone who has never experienced them, I found them very boring. For example, I guarded a door on the campus of the University of North Carolina for nearly three hours, waiting for President Nixon to come through the doorway. Such duty could be extremely uninteresting.

On the other hand, getting to know some of the Secret Service agents was very interesting, especially some of those with many years of experience.

The following stories, which I definitely cannot verify, and which must be consigned to the category of "rumor," were told to me by Secret Service agents who had been assigned to various Presidents and Vice-Presidents over a period of many years.

The most interesting of these tales concerned President Lyndon Johnson. They were related by a former agent who served for many years as a personal bodyguard to Mr. Johnson when he was Vice-President and President.

This agent was with Vice-President Johnson at a rally in Texas when he delivered his world-famous pro-civil rights speech from an outdoor platform in 100° heat. The platform was crowded with many dignitaries, including several prominent Black politicians. During the speech Johnson released tons of rhetoric in praise of the Black race. He made radical promises such as "making up for the 200 years of discrimination suffered by our brothers of color," and so forth.

According to the agent, when the speech was completed and the multitude of microphones were turned off, Johnson loosened his collar and tie and uttered loudly, "Now get them stinking niggers out of my sight."

\* \* \*

At some point after Johnson became President, he was receiving a rubdown, lying on his stomach in the White House health club. According to the agent who was there, a courier came in and announced that he had a message for the President.

"Read it to me, son," ordered Johnson.

The message was that Bobby Baker, a very close associate of Johnson, had just been indicted by a federal grand jury in Virginia. Without even looking up, Johnson said, "Oh, hell, if that son-of-a-bitch talks, we'll all go to jail!"

\* \* \*

The President's daughter Lynda Bird was the object of a photo-op in the White House at which her engagement to Marine Captain Charles Robb was announced. After the festivities, those attending enjoyed champagne and a gab-fest. Johnson put an arm around the shoulders of Captain Robb and said, "Son, you ain't already fuckin' my little girl, are you?"

\* \* \*

Former agents who have worked close to Presidents do not mind rating them in one important category—that is, their attitude or pleasantness towards lowly servants such as bodyguards. Based on my conversations with others and my limited experience in working with our presidents, I will relate my opinion as to how they rate in this consideration.

An ATF agent I worked with in the Carolinas had previously worked for several years in Washington, D.C. as a member of the National Park Police. One of his duties was to accompany President Harry Truman on his famous early morning walks. The President was known to be blunt and feisty, but apparently only in situations requiring bluntness and sharp words.

According to my friend, Mr. Truman was a genuine pleasure to work with, very friendly and considerate of the "little people. " Mr. Truman did not appear to have the monumental ego that is possessed by literally everyone else who reaches the position of President of the United States. He once said, "If you live in Washington, D.C. and want a true friend, buy a dog!"

\* \* \*

Born rich and handsome, President John F. Kennedy had the potential to be a snobbish son of a bitch. Not so! He was very civil and down to earth, very likable and pleasant to serve. He is reputed to have said to an agent as they walked through a shopping mall, "Say, lend me $20, there's something I want to buy. Someone will pay you back." And someone always did. The President never had money with him, although the Kennedy family had more money than God.

\* \* \*

President Eisenhower's lifelong military tradition of protocol carried over into the presidency. Literally all that served him were considered inferior. Yet I only recall one "rumor" of his abuse of a Secret Service agent, that occurring on a golf course in Georgia. Eisenhower was said to have hit a ball near the bank of a creek. As he prepared to hit the ball, the soil started to crumble, causing the agent to fear that the President would fall into the creek. Instinctively the agent grabbed Eisenhower to prevent a fall. The President is alleged to have said, "Keep your goddam hands off me!"

\* \* \*

The only other tale concerning President Eisenhower that I know of was merely a comment comparing his effectiveness as a great military leader with that of being president. When someone asked his thoughts on that, his response was, "When I was the Supreme Commander of Allied Forces in Europe during World War II, I had dozens of generals and hundreds of colonels under my command. All I had to do was make a decision, give an order to a subordinate, and it would immediately be carried out. As President, I would make a decision, give the order to a subordinate, and sometimes discover a year or more later that no one had paid a damn bit of attention to it!"

Ross Perot has said, "Any person that is really qualified to be President of the United States would not have the job!" Who could blame them? After all, there is no room for advancement

\* \* \*

In my personal opinion, the champion of cordiality among presidents or presidential candidates was George Wallace, former Governor of Alabama. He was a real "law and order" person and always very pleasant to law enforcement personnel.

Tales of this sort, though not applauded by many people, do tend to show that our so-called elite are as ordinary as the rest of us and should not be expected to be perfect.

# POST-RETIREMENT

"How about that big cabin cruiser over there?" I asked the robust woman who owned the Happy Duck Boat Sales company.

"Thirty foot inboard, one marine engine Chris Craft, old but in perfect condition, only 600 hours on it. It's too big for a ski-boat, not fast enough to race, and not the ideal fishing boat," she replied.

"What's it used for, then?" I asked.

"Party boat, man, party boat! It sleeps six and fucks twelve!" I paid $4,000 for it.

Many people have asked, "What does a man like you do after retirement? Surely you will want to leave a legacy." My answer is "I've already created more legacy than I can apologize for the rest of my life."

Finding an interesting and contented lifestyle to engage in after twenty-four years of rough and tumble law enforcement is not easy.

Options are numerous. Travel? No. I've already been everywhere. Golf? Couldn't hit a bull in the ass with a bass fiddle, let alone a golf club. Politics? Nope!

Friends asked me to run for Congress. Told them I'd rather have VD than to be in Congress. Too, I couldn't get elected. Fishing? Not interested. Besides that, I don't eat anything that swims, creeps, crawls or climbs trees.

When I was a bachelor, that left girls, liquor and poker. For some reason however even that option did not have real appeal. I suppose it's because I've "been there, done that."

I did get involved in a form of gambling, or more accurately described as Russian Roulette namely the New York stock market. To my great surprise and good luck I did quite well. Enough so that I have paid more back to the government via capital gains taxes than it has paid me.

Many people who have survived an action-packed career resolve to write a book. Most never get around to doing it. I did. *Damn the Allegators* was published in 1989 via vanity publishing, meaning I paid to have it published. (Anyone can write a book that way.) I was surprised at its success, as it sold out three printings. Still I didn't make any money on it, and didn't really expect to. I did it for fun.

The fun part was the many TV appearances, newspaper and magazine interview requests. One was from a writer for *Road and Track* magazine, Mr. Alex Gabbard. It led to a very pleasant experience. He asked me to participate in the filming of a re-creation of the route used by Robert Mitchum's character in the movie "Thunder Road", from Harlan, Kentucky, to Knoxville, Tennessee. He asked that I attempt to find some operational cars of the make and model commonly used by moonshiners to transport illegal whiskey in the 1940's, 1950's, and 1960's.

Having been stationed in North Wilkesboro, N.C. for two tours during my career in the 50's and 60's, I went there to search for the type of automobiles that we would need. At that time the area was known far and wide as the Moonshine Capital of the World.

After contacting an old friend I was directed to a farm owned by a retired moonshiner, Willie Clay Call. I was amazed to find that he had two buildings filled with the exact type of vehicles that I was looking for. The collection included a score of 1940 Ford Coupes, which was the universally preferred favorite of drivers in that era, and several other models, each restored to mint condition with super racing engines and other features.

Willie Call was very friendly and extremely cooperative. He quickly volunteered to accompany me, use several of his cars at no cost, and to participate with Alex Gabbard as an adviser, which he did thereby assuring that the project was successful.

Willie Call was the very life of the effort. Something about him seemed familiar and I mentioned this fact to him.

"By God," he said, "I ought to look familiar to you, I went to prison twice, and you're the son-of-a-bitch that sent me both times." Then, of course I remembered him. I had seized his brand-new 1960 Dodge liquor car with all kind of special stuff on it including the fastest racing engine I had ever driven. Oh, yes! I loved that car! After I seized it and it was forfeited to the U.S. Government it was assigned to me as an official investigative car. It was the fastest car I have ever seen. So hot that hell wouldn't hold it!

Thus because of working together on this project, two old adversaries became friends. Willie invited me to visit him again, and said that he would arrange a meeting with the famous race driver Junior Johnson. I had not seen Junior since I had arrested him for running a monster still many years before. He went to prison for three years in the case.

As he had promised, Willie Clay went with me to Junior Johnson's home and racing headquarters in the Ingle Hollow section of Wilkes County, the exact area where I had arrested him years before for running the big distillery. I had purchased a little model copper distillery which I took along to give to Junior. I told him that it was to replace the one that we blew up when he was arrested. I asked him if he remembered me. "I won't ever forget you, I thought of you every night when I was in prison!" he replied.

Junior was very cordial and showed me through his million-dollar racing facility. He has made a huge success of his racing organization and of himself. He is famous throughout the world.

On the occasion of our visit, we had photographs made of all persons present, including several associates of his that I remembered as violators of the U.S. Liquor Laws. One of those photos is included herein.

**L to R: Willie Clay Call, Joe Carter and Junior Johnson**

# EPILOGUE

Many successful law enforcement officers learn that they must fight fire with fire at times. They are placed in a position of doing a difficult, and sometimes impossible, job while being hamstrung with antiquated constitutional amendments, emasculating court orders, bureaucratic bungling and beautifully designed and professionally stacked legal loopholes.

A good officer must have talents in the field of law enforcement approaching that of a lawyer, psychologist and minister, and at the same time be a physical marvel and con artist. He takes the chances of having his guts shot out and of losing his family because of prolonged absences from home.

Virtually all good officers have violated the laws in a technical sense, with no corrupt motives, in order to better enforce the statutes and by-pass unnecessary government regulations and procedures.

We could sit on our asses and do little. But crime would proliferate much more than it does now and more people would be murdered, raped, robbed and paralyzed in fear. Or we can take the long chances and do the best job. If we get by with it, we are heroes, which to the honorable officer means little. But it does mean a lot to know that we have accomplished our mission and made the country a safer place to live. It is self-satisfying and its own reward.

If we get caught with our hands in the cookie jar, we suffer. Supervisors who have been through it understand. But the news media, the headhunters and the prosecutors do not understand or else they think only of their own bag.

I'm not saying that the investigator, whether he be AT'F, Secret Service, FBI, SBI, or otherwise, constantly violates a law in order to better enforce the laws. This is the exception rather than the rule. But it is done.

An ATF agent who makes efforts comparable to the main characters in this book, should be entitled to retirement after ten years with full pay, like federal judges enjoy.

The most demoralizing factor, leaving most devastation in its wake, is the shameful failure of some judges, including federal judges, who brazenly acquit or slap a big shot moonshiner on the wrist at times laughing and joking with him in open court, giving him, in effect, no sentence. Then thirty minutes later, they send some poor bastard who has no money to prison for five to ten years for the exact same crime. Even worse is for the agent to work his heart out for months to build a good case against a big criminal and then see him never even go to court.

Incredibly, I have even seen a federal judge sentence such a criminal to stand up in court and shake hands with the officer who made the case against him, and promise to never violate the law again!

In another case, a criminal had shot at an officer and missed, although his intention was to kill. He was charged with assault, convicted and placed on a suspended sentence. The judge told him in open court: "Son, I'm going to place you on probation, but I'm here to tell you, if you had killed that officer, I would have been forced to send you to prison." FORCED!

I am thankful that I performed my duties without having to take the life of anyone, although I have walked into the barrels of shotguns and pistols and have taken knives from the hands of dangerous suspects. I have never owned a blackjack and never hit but two people with anything except my fists. Fists I have used and used effectively, but never without justification.

I have been injured eleven times, suffered two brain concussions and many broken bones, been shot at on many occasions, and also battered seriously in several automobile chases By the grace of God, I survived it all.

For many years I worked in districts where the courts destroyed all my efforts and the money that the U.S. Government spent went for naught. This contributed to the fatal demoralization of a strong spirit. The last year, my efforts were not worth a damn. My health had deteriorated to the point where I could no longer keep up. Thus, I retired, but if I had to live the time over, I would do exactly the same thing!